Here's a clear, creative, and compelling case for how to deal with the cultural conflicts that threaten to tear us apart, and instead to find the foundation for our humanity that can give us the common ground we need. This book will stimulate your thinking, engage your imagination, and ultimately change the way you see others—and even how you view yourself!

—LEE STROBEL, bestselling author; director, The Lee Strobel Center, Colorado Christian University

Only by looking through Christ's eyes can you see the real value of human life, and only by putting on Christ's heart can you love the broken human being. This book will help you to critically think, "What is the value of human life?"

—SOKREAKSA HIMM, survivor of Cambodia's Killing Fields; author, *The Tears of My Soul* and *After the Heavy Rain*

This is a timely and powerful book. We have lost sight of what a human is because we have lost sight of God. Ultimately, this book is a call to better love our neighbors by understanding the faulty worldview that takes so many people captive today.

—SEAN MCDOWELL, professor, Talbot School of Theology; coauthor, *Evidence That Demands a Verdict.*

This book allows us to think about what it means to be human and what it means to dehumanize others. It needs to be on the shelf of every Christian thinker.

—GEORGE YANCEY, professor of sociology, Baylor University

I warmly commend this book and its goal of pointing people to the God in relationship with whom we become truly human. We have never lived in a time like this, and this book has never been more important.

—JUSTIN BR̶ editor, Premi̶ ̶vable?

Our culture often devalues children, especially those with a disability. This book is a timely reminder that how we see people affects how we treat them. I highly recommend it to make sure you are seeing people correctly.

—JONG-RAK LEE, pastor, Jusarang Church Community,
featured in *The Drop Box* documentary

I spent most of my career assigned to a Crimes Persons unit as a detective in Los Angeles County. It doesn't take long in this environment to witness the disregard humans have for one another. But while homicides represent an extreme expression of our growing intolerance, a more insidious divide widens between us as our culture abandons its Christian foundation. This book describes this danger and calls us to the one solution that can restore our sense of common humanity.

—J. WARNER WALLACE, senior fellow, Colson
Center for Christian Worldview; adjunct professor
of apologetics, Talbot School of Theology

The arguments that Andy Steiger makes in this book are essential to understanding our cultural moment as we continue that profoundly human quest for truth and meaning. Steiger helps us to reset and to remember the importance of genuine human community.

—REV. DR. ANDREW BENNETT, director,
Cardus Religious Freedom Institute

Once you start reading this book, you will have difficulty putting it down. Its stories will draw you in, and its blend of philosophical reasoning and theological insights will make you think about some of the deepest questions one could ever ask: What is it to be human? What leads to human flourishing? And why is it so devastating when we dehumanize others?

—PAUL CHAMBERLAIN, professor of ethics and
leadership, and director, Institute of Christian
Apologetics, Trinity Western University

In this secular age in which we know the cost of everything but the value of nothing, it is imperative we thoughtfully consider the ideas in this book. To a society that has given up introspection and given in to daily distractions, this book ought to help reverse cultural malaise. I highly recommend it.

—HARRY EDWARDS, founder and
director, Apologetics.com, Inc.

Using vivid illustrations and spellbinding stories to make his important case, Andy has written a book in which philosophy, anthropology, and the Bible collide in beautiful ways to reveal genuine human flourishing. Church leaders and school teachers be aware: this book will enlighten and transform people at every age and of every race, gender, and educational background. Get everyone reading it today.

—CRAIG J. HAZEN, professor of comparative religion
and apologetics, Talbot School of Theology; author,
Five Sacred Crossings and *Fearless Prayer*

This timely book unpacks the consequences that follow when we forget what it means to be human, and it shows powerfully why only the Christian faith can give us a foundation for human value and dignity, a foundation based not in chemistry nor psychology nor biology but in the love of the God who made us and who, in Jesus, rescued and reclaimed our broken humanity.

—DR. ANDY BANNISTER, director, Solas Centre
for Public Christianity; adjunct speaker, Ravi
Zacharias International Ministries

All words are riddles that have to be unpacked. Today, the word human has become a cultural riddle with no clear meaning. Through compelling writing and arguments, Steiger offers a thoroughly biblical definition not only of what it means to be human but also how of to flourish.

—TIM MUEHLHOFF, professor of communication,
Biola University; author, *Winsome Persuasion:
Christian Influence in a Post-Christian World*

Andy Steiger's book alerts us to the looming dangers of dehumanization embedded within a naturalistic or atheistic worldview. He rightly anchors the hope of recognizing and reclaiming our humanity and personhood as presented in the biblical revelation and grounded in the triune God—the ultimate basis for deep relationality and intimacy.

—PAUL COPAN, Pledger Family Chair of Philosophy
and Ethics, Palm Beach Atlantic University;
coauthor, *An Introduction to Biblical Ethics*

In the height of colonization, our people witnessed a people who chose not to see us as a people and did not understand our relationship with Creator God. When I was young, the Indian Affairs agent would come to our community, and our people would go to great lengths to honor him. I could not understand this action. My mother said, "It doesn't matter what they are doing to us, we must always respect all people because God made them also." This book opens the gate to reclaim our birthright as a people of God, made in his image.

—CHIEF KENNY BLACKSMITH

RECLAIMED

RECLAIMED

HOW JESUS RESTORES OUR HUMANITY
IN A DEHUMANIZED WORLD

ANDY STEIGER
WITH SHERI HIEBERT

ZONDERVAN
REFLECTIVE

DEDICATION

To my beautiful and brilliant wife, Nancy.
Over the years, we have been on many adventures
together, and you have always been my best friend
and greatest encouragement. I love you!

CONTENTS

ZOMBIE CULTURE

There I was, running down the city streets, surrounded by a horde of the undead. As zombies poured in from all directions, I had flashbacks to when I watched *Night of the Living Dead* as a teenager. That movie had freaked me out and now here I was, experiencing it. No, this wasn't a zombie apocalypse, a movie set, or a disturbing nightmare. It was the tenth annual Zombiewalk Vancouver held in British Columbia, Canada. Each year, thousands of the walking dead arrive at the Vancouver Art Gallery in costumes drenched in blood, brains, and gore that could rival those in the latest Hollywood blockbuster. A strange symphony of moans and groans fills the air as the zombies walk, limp, and drag their corpses the three kilometers to English Bay.

That year, I decided to witness this bizarre display of zombie devotion firsthand. I pulled on my green "Zombies Eat Flesh" T-shirt, grabbed a film crew, and headed down to the gruesome scene to conduct interviews with the zombie walkers. I've always found people's fascination with the undead interesting and wanted to better understand it.

About halfway through the zombie walk, we came upon a street preacher. He was perched atop a soapbox with a bullhorn in his hand. He was waving his Bible wildly in the air as he amplified his rebukes and attempted to cast the demons out of the people moaning past him. It was one of the most bizarre

1

scenes I've ever witnessed. Both the zombie walkers and the street preacher stared at each other in utter confusion. It was a striking visual depiction of two worldviews colliding.

I interviewed a lot of people that day, and the first question I asked each of them is, "What is a zombie?" Not a single person agreed with the street preacher, who thought of zombies as demonic. Demons are spiritual creatures with cunning minds and sinister personalities. Universally, people define a zombie as just the opposite: as an empty human body devoid of personhood, mind, or soul. I followed up that question by asking, "Well, what's a human then?" Each person looked exactly like a zombie as they stared at me, their mind totally blank. The irony hit even them. I was speaking to humans pretending to be zombies who had spent much more time thinking about their fantasy than about their reality. They knew that they were different from zombies, were more than mindless bodies, but they couldn't tell me how they knew that or what made them different.

I often think about that zombie walk and what those blank stares revealed: our culture is deeply confused about what it means to be human. Never has humanity been so connected across the globe. People on all points of the political spectrum and from all walks of life share a deep desire for a better world, a world that upholds human rights and dignity. Yet we're uncertain how to achieve this aim because we don't have answers to basic questions about our humanity: What is human? What is the value of human life? What leads to human flourishing? How should humans live?

These questions are the driving force behind many of our most popular TV shows and movies. They are the permanent backdrop to our news stories and political issues. Questions about human dignity are motivating many of our culture's most important conversations about race, gender, scientific research, social media, and human pain and suffering. Yet despite a culture that pays lip service to tolerance, it's actually becoming more and more difficult to look past our differences and see our common humanity. That's what makes zombies so disturbing. They are a visual representation of a gruesome reality—the dehumanization we are all capable of when we lose sight of another person's humanity. The way we treat each other is a result of how we see one another, and our culture is full of warning signs that we aren't seeing each other's humanity correctly. The reality of what we are capable of when we dehumanize is far worse than any horror flick.

I believe that our culture has lost sight of what a human is because we have lost sight of God.

We live in a culture that has removed God from nearly every sphere of life. God has been erased from our education, employment, politics, health, sexuality, finances, and even religion. Everything! Western culture has exiled God from reality, happy to relegate him to the realm of therapeutic fairy tales. The problem is that without God, we lose the answers to important questions of who we are, what we are worth, and what leads to the best life. Without God, there are no firm answers to these questions. Instead, the best we can do is offer up a mixed bag of personal opinions and ever-changing societal values.

The Bible's answer teaches us that in order to see our humanity, we first need to see God. God is most clearly seen in Jesus Christ. It's only through Jesus that we can see both God's nature and our nature. Through Jesus, we find that humans are unique, valuable, and bearers of rights and responsibilities. However, we don't live that truth. Instead, we indulge our dehumanizing tendencies by rejecting God and everything he says about who we are. Yet God doesn't abandon us. His son, Jesus, lived amid our brokenness and witnessed our inclination toward inhumanity. Because of his death and resurrection, our humanity can be reclaimed. Jesus enables us to be fully human, and it's in him that we rediscover the kind of relationships and society for which so many people today are longing.

In this book, each pair of chapters addresses one of the four fundamental questions about humanity: What is a human? What is the value of human life? What leads to human flourishing? How should humans live? Each pair will explore how answering the question without God leads to a dehumanized world and how restoring God to our worldview leads to a humanized world.

Now more than ever, we need to see our humanity and the humanity of others. Only in Jesus can this take place. Jesus is the foundation for rediscovering our common ground and our shared humanity in a dehumanized culture.

PART 1

WHAT IS HUMAN?

DIGITAL GENOCIDE

It was a beautiful June afternoon, and although I had just gotten home from work, the bright sunshine compelled me to stay outside and mow the lawn. I had just pulled out the lawn mower and was firing it up when my wife and kids pulled into the driveway. With tears in her eyes, my wife flew out of the car and ran up the lawn toward me. The story spilled out of her: an accusatory post about me had appeared on Facebook, sparking a campaign against me. A mere fifteen minutes after the posting, before I was even aware of the issue, I had been officially uninvited from speaking at a local high school. There was even talk that the teacher who invited me could lose her job or the school could be sued because of me.

As a pastor, I am frequently asked to speak at local high schools and universities on a variety of topics. This time, I had been asked to speak to a grade-twelve class on dehumanization. The class had invited speakers from different world religions, and I was to represent the Christian perspective on dehumanization, explaining how Jesus lays a foundation for humanization. It seemed like a perfect fit, given that my PhD work was on that topic and that a film I had recently created on dehumanization, called *The Human Project,* had won a number of awards.[1] I had accepted the speaking request months earlier, and the parents had all been notified that I was coming. I was looking forward to sharing my research and experience on the topic and engaging with the students. Now, it had all come to an abrupt halt the night before I was scheduled to speak.

My heart sank. "Why?" I asked.

"Because of the podcast you did," my wife replied.

The podcast was an interview I had hosted about a new public-school curriculum to support gender diversity among elementary school students. I had learned that not everyone in the transgender community supported this new curriculum, so naturally I was curious why. I invited a trans-identified male on my show and had a wonderful conversation discussing his concerns about the curriculum. Although he is openly transgender and is not a Christian, the LGBTQ community despised him for openly challenging the curriculum. This new online response to the podcast showed me I had failed to appreciate just how hated this man was and how intolerant our culture had become to differences of opinion. Now this hatred was being directed at me.

In the post and its resulting comments section, people had grabbed random statements from my website and other podcasts I had done and quoted them out of context in an attempt to show what a horrible person I am. Clearly, none of these people knew who I was or what I thought. My name wasn't even spelled correctly. Apparently, there's a guy out there named Andy Steigler you should all watch out for.

The post argued that I and the religion I represented should never be allowed in a public school. Dozens of people chimed in. Some risked supporting me, and others hurled insults, accusing me of bigotry, fanaticism, and brainwashing kids. In the end, the school labeled me unsafe. I was told that the students might not feel comfortable hearing from me. How ironic, I thought. I had been asked to speak on how Christianity allows us to love and humanize each other. It was a topic to which I had devoted not only my academic study but also my entire life as a pastor. Yet in only fifteen minutes, I had been reduced to a caricature and vilified as dangerous. Dehumanization, the very topic that this class was studying, was taking place right before the students' eyes.

HATEBOOK

Dehumanization happens when we see others as less than human. Separating people into groups and then stirring up fear is the quintessence of dehumanization. What happened to me that day in June was small and had minimal consequences. But multiply that interaction by thousands or even millions of people and the consequences change. It's these small, dehumanizing moments that ultimately form huge cultural movements like what happened in Rwanda or Nazi Germany. If you think such large-scale dehumanization is a thing of the past, think again. In the twenty-first century, nowhere has the path to dehumanization been more evident than in the country of Myanmar.

Myanmar is a predominantly Buddhist country that gained independence from the British in 1948. Since the days of colonial rule, the Buddhist Burmese people have harbored an intense hatred of and discrimination toward the Rohingya people, a small Muslim minority. For decades, the Rohingya have been denied citizenship in Myanmar. They have been denied the opportunity to own land, have children freely, or even travel to the next village. They have been forced to live in camps set apart from the rest of the population, where they don't have access to education, health care, or even proper food and water. Those things are horrible in themselves, but things have gotten worse in the past few years, and the dehumanization is now spilling over into horrific violence. As of December 2018, the United Nations, the United States House of Representatives, and the United States Holocaust Memorial Museum have all released statements confirming that genocide is taking place in Myanmar. A UN fact-finding mission in the fall of 2018 found that the crimes being committed against the Rohingya include systematic mass killings, mass public gang rapes, burning of villages, forced labor, torture, and regular unexplained disappearances.

The situation in Myanmar is rightly being compared to the genocide in Rwanda in the 1990s and the genocide of Jews in 1940s Europe. In Nazi Germany, oppressors used books, pamphlets, and speeches to spread dehumanization and stir the people to violence. In Rwanda, they used radio. In Myanmar, they use something that hits a little too close to home: Facebook.

In 2012, only 1 percent of the people living in Myanmar had access to the internet.[2] On a world ranking of mobile phone users, Myanmar ranked second last, just above North Korea. Yet everything changed in 2013. Swift political changes opened the country to foreign telecommunications companies and everything exploded. Only four years later, the price of SIM cards had plunged by 99 percent and half the people in Myanmar had mobile phones. Most people were using only one app: Facebook. Cell phone companies had been offering sign-up bonuses that let users avoid data charges when using Facebook, and in a poor country like Myanmar that was a game changer. For a huge portion of the population, Facebook became the sum total of the internet.[3] But rather than trivial status updates or pictures of people's pets, in Myanmar Facebook had become a festering ground for racial hatred and calls to violence. Both the Myanmar military and a prominent group of monks called the Ma Ba Tha have led the charge, spreading anti-Muslim hate speech on social media. Crude memes perpetuate the idea that the Muslim Rohingya are violent and both a danger to the Burmese people and a threat to Burmese racial and religious purity. Monks call for their followers to respond to these threats, and so they do and people die.

Notice what happened to me online and what is happening to the Rohingya online. Both are examples of dehumanization. One is so minimal it's hardly worth mentioning, and the other is extreme and should be shouted from the rooftops, but both stem from the same root. On Facebook, I was no longer seen as a flesh-and-blood human, a husband and father, but was instead reduced to a stereotype and assumed to be a certain way. I was labeled unsafe and denied the opportunity to speak at a school. On Facebook, the Rohingya are also no longer seen as flesh-and-blood humans, husbands and fathers, and instead are reduced to stereotypes and assumed to be a certain way. However, when they are labeled unsafe, they aren't just denied the opportunity to speak but are denied the right to life. That's not as big of a bridge to cross as you'd think.

LESS THAN HUMAN

It might be tempting to think that atrocities like the one in Myanmar are isolated to certain cultures, geographical locations, or times, but they're not. During the twentieth century alone, genocides took place all over the globe, including in Argentina, Turkey, Germany, Cambodia, Iraq, Bosnia, Russia, and Rwanda. If you expand your consideration to include all types of crimes against humanity throughout history—war, terrorism, torture, rape, racism, and slavery—the scope is truly staggering. There is no group of people on the planet that has not been affected. So how can people be capable of such heinous crimes against one another? The answer is consistent: dehumanization.

Dehumanization is not an optional step on the path to harming each other; it is a necessary step. The truth is that people rarely murder people. That may seem like an odd claim, but before you dismiss it, let's think about it. First, let me clarify what I am not saying. Notice that I didn't say that people do not *kill* people. Clearly, that happens all the time. People do accidentally kill other people, like in a car crash, or someone might kill another person in self-defense. What I'm talking about here is murder—the malicious act of taking another person's life. That's just not something people do to other people. Instead, the easiest way to murder, on a large scale or small, is to no longer see them as people at all. This is the power of dehumanization. It enables one's ability to murder by distorting how one perceives the person they're murdering. To our eyes it may look like people murder *people,* but that's often not how murderers see it. In their minds, whether or not it's a conscious thought, they see the other person as less than human.

The power of dehumanization was clearly documented in a BBC program on the creation of the Auschwitz death camp. In the summer of 1941, when Auschwitz had not yet become a factory of death, the Germans organized mobile killing units in Eastern Europe. Groups of soldiers rounded up Jews, dug massive pits, and then shot the men, women, and children, watching as their dying bodies fell into the mass grave. The documentary showed an interview with a man named Hans Friedrich, who had been a soldier during this time and participated in shooting Jews point blank. The interviewer asked a question that most people familiar with the barbarism of the Holocaust struggle to comprehend: "Can you tell me what you were thinking and feeling when you were shooting?" His answer was a chilling reminder of the effectiveness of dehumanization. He replied, "Nothing," and then continued, "I only thought: Aim carefully, so that you hit properly. That was my thought." The interviewer, clearly frustrated by Friedrich's lack of emotion, asked, "This was your only thought? During all that time you had no feelings for the people, the Jewish civilians, that you shot?" He took a deep shaky breath and then replied, "No."[4]

I was outraged! How can that be? If you've ever seen Holocaust photographs of emaciated children and adults who have been starved, stripped naked, and murdered en masse, then you can understand the wickedness of these crimes. Yet, apparently, this man felt nothing! It is almost beyond belief. However, I've come to realize that asking a Nazi what it felt like to shoot the Jews is like asking an exterminator what they were thinking and feeling while eliminating an infestation of rats. As professor Claudia Koonz explains, "Nazi public culture was constructed on the mantra: 'Not every being with a human face is a human.'"[5]

Oskar Gröning, a Nazi convicted of war crimes in 2015 at age ninety-three for his participation at Auschwitz, explained how the Holocaust was possible, saying, "We were convinced by our *worldview* that we had been betrayed by the entire world and that there was a great conspiracy of the Jews against us."[6] A worldview is the way you see and understand the world; it's a culturally prescriptive lens that is crafted by your beliefs and experiences. Like most Nazis, Gröning was convinced that the world, and especially the Jews, was against them. Nazi propaganda only strengthened the belief that Jews, and others, were no longer persons in the same way that Germans were. When you no longer see a person, you become capable of acting on your evil desires of murder, rape, slavery—you name it.

Philosopher David Livingstone Smith articulates it this way: "Subhumans, it was believed, are beings that lack that special something that makes us human. Because of this deficit, they don't command the respect that *we*, the truly human beings, are obliged to grant one another. They can be enslaved, tortured, or even exterminated—treated in ways in which we could not bring ourselves to treat those whom we regard as members of our own kind."[7]

If you could go back in time and ask a Nazi who participated in the genocide whether murdering people is wrong, they likely would answer, "Yes! Of course murdering people is wrong. But Jews are not people." A Hutu man convicted of murdering Tutsis during the genocide in Rwanda illustrated this point, saying, "We no longer saw a human being when we turned up a Tutsi in the swamps. I mean a person like us, sharing similar thoughts and feelings."[8]

Now, please don't confuse an explanation with an excuse. I'm not arguing that Nazis' and Hutus' blindness to another's humanity justifies their actions. It does not. My point is simply to show that these unfathomable actions are perhaps not so unfathomable after all.

UNBRIDLED

It's frightening to realize, but once our perspective of others becomes twisted, our actions eventually follow suit. One clear indicator of how we see others is the words we use. During World War II, the Nazis called the Jews "rats," the Japanese called the Chinese "insects," and Americans called the Japanese "monkeys." During the Rwandan genocide, the Hutus called the Tutsis "cockroaches" and "snakes." Even farther back, the Spanish conquistadors called the Native Americans "talking animals" and "soulless parrots in human guise."

But let's not kid ourselves. In the twenty-first century, are we any better?

Today in Myanmar, they call the Rohingya people "Kalars," a derogatory term referencing their skin color and foreignness. Take a moment to see if you can think of dehumanizing labels *we* use for people of a different race, size, gender, sexual orientation, education, political view, or religion. I'm sure it didn't take you long. Most are too foul to mention, and sadly we're all guilty. We may not think too deeply about what we call people, but these are more than mere words. They are indicative of how we see people and how we will treat them if we view them through these lenses.

Writing in the first century, James, the brother of Jesus Christ, challenged how we talk about people. In a letter that James wrote to churches, he says, "All kinds of animals, birds, reptiles and sea creatures are being tamed and have been tamed by mankind, but no human being can tame the tongue. It is a restless evil, full of deadly poison. With the tongue we praise our Lord and Father, and with it we curse human beings, who have been made in God's likeness. Out of the same mouth come praise and cursing. My brothers and sisters, this should not be."[9]

Nowhere is the poison of the human tongue more potent than in its ability to put people down. We've all experienced it, and worse, we've all done it. But how do we change?

The first step to restoring another's humanity is to diagnose the problem. We need first to understand dehumanization and learn to spot it in ourselves and others. However, this can be a real challenge given the creative lengths we often go to when demeaning others. The difficulty we have in uprooting dehumanizing language can be illustrated with the history of the slur "Monday." Monday is a day of the week, an innocent word if there ever was one, and yet in 2012 a police officer in New Hampshire was fired for using Monday as a derogatory term for a member of the Boston Red Sox. Many people were understandably confused. But the connection had been explained in the media in 2008, when stand-up comedian Russell Peters performed a routine in which he described a confusing conversation he had with a man from Boston. The man had referred to black people as Mondays and when Peters questioned what that meant, the man casually explained, "Because nobody likes Mondays."[10]

Now, Peters is a professional comedian and he played the situation for laughs, but the real purpose of his routine was to bring to light a more sinister reality: our derogatory terms might be more covert or camouflaged than in years past, but that's not a credit to our growing kindness. It's just an indication of our growing cleverness. As the *Boston Globe* pointed out in an article on the Red Sox incident, "The history of such secret slurs teaches an important lesson: Words can always be weaponized."[11] We like to think that as a culture we have improved since the time of the conquistadors or the Nazis, yet at no time in history has this truth about the weaponization of words been more evident than in the twenty-first century, when our dehumanizing inclination has discovered a new global playground: the internet.

ADD A PUBLIC COMMENT

Social media has become a war-torn wasteland of digital genocide. The digital era presents a unique challenge because never has it been so easy to delete another's humanity. From the comfort, convenience, and privacy of your home, the unbridled tongue is free to type and unleash its full poison on whomever you choose without ever looking them in the face. Consider how easy it is to type the unfiltered thoughts of your heart into 140 characters and press Send. You don't need to see or hear the human being on the other end. You don't need to face the fallout of the bombs you drop.

My experience with internet harassment was disturbing and unpleasant, but the long-term effects were minimal. Unfortunately, that's not the case for thousands, maybe millions, of people online. In his book *So You've Been Publicly Shamed*, Jon Ronson tells the stories of people whose lives have been destroyed by vicious social media beatings. These were normal people who made a mistake online, be it a joke in bad taste or a poorly worded tweet, and were subsequently demolished, receiving tens of thousands of cruel, violent, and threatening messages in return. Not only that, the vicious side of social-media shaming has caused many to be fired from their jobs and to lose relationships with friends and loved ones, and even has led some to commit suicide. One woman tweeted, "Going to Africa. Hope I don't get AIDS. Just kidding. I'm white!" before boarding her flight, and by the time she landed, she had lost her job and her humiliation was the number-one topic on Twitter.[12] Your insensitive joke used to earn you an eye-roll or a swat from your friends at a party, but eventually it would be forgotten. You could learn from your mistake and move on with your life. Now, on social media that low moment can have an audience of millions and will be enshrined in internet history, where nothing is ever truly deleted and no one ever lets you forget. Nobody's perfect, and yet on the internet you'd better be, or watch out.

Nowadays my preservation instincts have taught me to turn off the comments function online and to avoid discussion threads about controversial topics. The internet is humanity's reminder that we can't have nice things. It exposes the broken-ness of the human heart. Consider how different it would be if we were required to meet someone face-to-face before posting. What if you were required to read or hear a short biography of the person behind the tweet before you posted your comment? I know this suggestion is not practical, but it highlights the power of humanization. When you humanize a person, it isn't nearly so easy to verbally tear them apart.

Writer Lindy West discovered this firsthand when she decided to respond to some online harassment. Her articles about feminism, body image, and social justice regularly inspired hate-filled backlash from what she called her "trolls." Mostly she tried to have a thick skin and ignore it. Blocking users on her Twitter account became a part of her daily (or hourly) life.

Then one tweet showed up that found a chink in her armor. It was a cruel message from her much-loved and bitterly grieved dead father. Yes, someone had decided to research her family, read the obituary Lindy had written, and then make a fake account. It was the worst comment she had ever received and it was viciously personal. Why would someone do that? Not content to just ignore it like usual, she decided to respond. She wrote an article for the online magazine she worked for, talking about internet trolling and relaying the message she had gotten from her "dad." A few hours later, she got the strangest email of her life. It was from her troll, who admitted to everything and apologized. He said, "I can't say sorry enough. It was the lowest thing I had ever done. When you included it in your latest article, it finally hit me. There is a living, breathing human being who is reading this." A few months later, he even agreed to conduct a phone interview with her for a popular radio show. They ended up having a good conversation in which they discussed the motives for his actions and she ended up feeling surprised at how normal he was and how talking to him made her anger dissipate. "This story isn't prescriptive," she concluded. "It doesn't mean that anyone is obliged to forgive people who abuse them, or even that I plan on being cordial and compassionate to every teenage boy who pipes up to call me a blue whale. But, for me, it's changed the timbre of my online interactions . . . It's hard to feel hurt or frightened when you're flooded with pity. It's hard to be cold or cruel when you remember it's hard to be a person . . . I can remember not to lose sight of their humanity the way that they lost sight of mine."[13]

THE MONSTER WITHIN

These modern examples of dehumanization challenge us not to make the mistake of believing that the Hutus who participated in the Rwandan genocide, the Nazis who committed the Holocaust, or the Burmese who are harming the Rohingya today are unique monsters, exceptions in a world of mostly normal people. It's comforting to assume that acting on a dehumanizing perspective is something that only a few broken people are capable of, certainly not me. After all, the internet isn't real life, right? I might use nasty words about people, but it's just a joke. I would never actually treat someone that way.

It's a reassuring thought, yet ultimately it's a fantasy. Study after study has been done on dehumanization and the capacity for human cruelty, and the results are always the same: no one is immune. Dehumanization is a blindness that we are all easily capable of acting on with terrifying results. A Rwandan survivor confirms this, saying, "Now I know that even the person with whom you've shared food, or with whom you've slept, even he can kill you with no trouble. The closest neighbor can kill you with his teeth: that is what I have learned since the genocide, and my eyes no longer gaze the same on the face of the world."[14]

The history of human violence has shown that ordinary people, no matter their level of education, are capable of truly terrible acts once their perspective of another's humanity is twisted. When Adolf Eichmann, an organizer of the Holocaust, was put on trial in Jerusalem in 1961, people expected to see a monster. Instead, they found something that inspired journalist Hannah Arendt to coin the term "the banality of evil."[15] In her book *Eichmann in Jerusalem,* Arendt writes, "[The judges] knew, of course, that it would have been very comforting indeed to believe that Eichmann was a monster, even though if he had been, Israel's case against him would have collapsed . . . The trouble with Eichmann was precisely that so many were like him, and the many were neither perverted nor sadistic, that they were, and still are, terribly and terrifyingly normal."

Journalist Slavenka Drakulić witnessed the trial for war crimes committed in the former Yugoslavia, where ethnic cleansing claimed the lives of more than a hundred thousand people and thousands were systematically raped, tortured, and enslaved. She expressed a similar insight:

> You sit in a courtroom watching a defendant day after day and at first you wonder, as Primo Levi did, "if this is a man." No, this is not a man, it is all too easy to answer, but as the days pass you find the criminals become increasingly human. Soon you feel that you know them intimately. You watch their faces, ugly or pleasant, their small habits of yawning, taking notes, scratching their heads, cleaning their nails, and you have to ask yourself: what if this *is* a man? The more you know them, the more you wonder how they could have committed such crimes, these waiters and taxi drivers, teachers and peasants in front of you. And the more you realize that war criminals might be ordinary people, the more afraid you become. Of course, this is because the consequences are more serious than if they were monsters. If ordinary people committed war crimes, it means that any of us can commit them. Now you understand why it is so easy and comfortable to accept that war criminals are monsters.[16]

The people who participated in genocide, rape, and torture were ordinary people. They were devoted husbands and wives and loving fathers and mothers, not the monsters one would imagine, given what they did. The brokenness of humanity is much deeper than we would like to think. The potential for truly monstrous deeds is in us all. The ability to act on that evil is unleashed by first erasing another's humanity.

SOUL SUICIDE

Remember how I argued that people do not murder people? Well, that statement can be read in one of two ways. So far, we've seen that people do not murder *people*—that you become capable of murdering a person's body or destroying their character only when you no longer see them as people at all. However, there is another possibility. It's also true to say that *people* do not murder people. To commit murder or even humiliate or belittle others, you first must dehumanize yourself.

One of the most chilling descriptions of the dehumanization of self is described by James Gilligan, an American psychiatrist. In the 1970s, he was hired by a prison in Massachusetts to help figure out why there was so much violence among its inmates. The brutality had escalated to an extreme level. Prisoners were murdering not only other prisoners but also guards and visitors, at the rate of one a month. They were even taking their own lives, with a suicide occurring every six weeks. After interviewing the violent offenders one after the other, a strange pattern emerged. Gilligan writes:

> The men would all say that they had died. These were the most incorrigibly violent characters. They would all say that they themselves had died before they started killing other people. What they meant was that their personalities had died. They felt dead inside . . . Some have told me that they feel like robots or zombies, that their bodies are empty or filled with straw, not flesh and blood, that instead of having veins and nerves they have ropes or cords. One inmate told me he feels like "food that is decomposing." These men's souls did not just die. They have dead souls because their souls were murdered.[17]

Did you notice how the men denied themselves human nature? Rather than seeing themselves as living beings with flesh and blood, they instead saw only dead, impersonal things: robots, zombies, straw, food, ropes. Before they murdered others or themselves, they lost sight of their humanity. Serial killer Ted Bundy made a similar confession. In an interview with James Dobson, days before his execution, he explained how he would use alcohol to take that final step in numbing his humanity before he could commit his heinous crimes.[18] Given the number of murders, rapes, and incidents of domestic abuse that are connected with alcohol and drug use, this shouldn't be surprising.

Although these are extreme examples, we are all capable, in varying degrees, of becoming numb to our humanity. I remember in high school when a friend told me that he wished he had never been born. I asked what he meant, and he explained that he didn't believe in God and he felt like meaningless DNA. In light of the inevitability of death and the challenges of life, he felt like just giving up and struggled with suicidal thoughts. I could sympathize with him, because I too had struggled with the weight of meaninglessness and its ability to kill the soul. It began when I was about twelve. Often at night when I was alone and about to fall asleep, the thought of dying would draw me into a black hole of dark thoughts. As I thought about the eternity of nothingness that awaited me in death, meaninglessness would overwhelm me until I was nauseated. My soul hurt, and as I aged I got better at learning how to distract myself from the dark thoughts. Things changed for me at seventeen when I found God. Actually, I had always believed that God existed, but I hadn't allowed that belief to inform my view of myself or other people. By failing to see my purpose and value, I was dehumanizing myself. When I became a Christian, my world changed. I changed. I went from seeing a gray world of meaninglessness to seeing a vibrant world of color, and for the first time I truly saw my humanity and the humanity of others.

How we see ourselves and others is an important aspect of evil that is often overlooked. The Bible explains that human desires are bent toward breaking relationships. It's what comes naturally to us. Restoring relationships does not. It's not only that we do wrong, it's that we want to do wrong. Part of our bentness comes in the form of a vision problem. How do you see yourself? How do you see others? If we don't see people correctly, or even want to see people correctly, we will not treat people correctly. The jump from a cruel tweet to genocide is a lot smaller than we would like to think, and maintaining a correct view of ourselves and others is a lot more difficult than we are willing to admit. We naturally feed our biases, and we live in a world where it is increasingly easy to do just that.

So how do we fix this problem?

After I was uninvited to speak at that high school, one of the students emailed me, saying that her class was shocked when they heard that I had been uninvited because someone had complained in a Facebook post. She apologized and asked if I would be willing to meet with her class off school property, because many of them still wanted to hear from me. The students had to arrange everything themselves, because the adults were concerned about losing their jobs and the school was still afraid of lawsuits.

Ironically, a church nearby was willing to offer the students space to host the meeting. We ate pizza in the foyer as I shared with the class my research on dehumanization. The question they were most curious about was the logical one: How do we stop it? How do we humanize?

As I've researched, I've realized that, despite being aware of the problem, historians and philosophers are at a loss for a solution. David Livingstone Smith makes this clear at the end of his book on dehumanization. He spends almost three hundred pages talking about the problem of dehumanization and less than one hundred words on the solution. All he has to say is, "The study of dehumanization needs to be made a priority. Universities, governments, and nongovernmental organizations need to put money, time, and talent into figuring out exactly how dehumanization works and what can be done to prevent it. Maybe then we can use this knowledge to build a future that is less hideous than our past: a future with no Rwandas, no Hiroshimas, and no Final Solutions. Can this be done? Nobody knows, because nobody's ever tried."[19]

It sounds nice, doesn't it? His words are hopeful and convicting. But if you look closer, his solution isn't really much of a solution after all. The truth is that we already know how dehumanization works. More academic study won't solve this issue because fundamentally, dehumanization is a heart problem. Because our desires are bent, our worldviews and perspectives are distorted.

As the students and I learned that day, talking with each other is a good start toward changing our perspective. Many of the students were surprised to see that I'm a normal guy. Some anticipated a religious fanatic and were a little afraid to come to the meeting. But talking face-to-face isn't the solution either. That day, I was able to share with them the real answer to dehumanization: Jesus. Only a relationship with Jesus can change our hearts and worldviews. Jesus is able to heal our brokenness by giving us his perspective and his desires so that we can see each other correctly and delight in the restoration of relationships.

CAGED BIRD IN BANGKOK

I can only imagine how Noi's mother must have felt as she stood in the rice field of their farm in Thailand and held a hand to her abdomen. Pregnant, again? They barely had enough money to look after their six children. The thought of another hungry mouth to feed must have made her tremble in despair. Feeling like she had no other choice, she made a decision that later haunted her. Only a couple of swallows, she was told, and she could be rid of this burden growing inside her. She grimaced as she drank the bitter liquid.

Nine months later, my friend Noi was born. The concoction her mother had taken didn't end Noi's life, but it did cause birth defects that affected every day of her life afterward. Noi's growth was severely stunted and one of her eyes was deformed. As a child, both her height and her eye acted as lightning rods for the cruelty of her classmates and neighbors. The insults and teasing were relentless. Despite the closeness of their farming community, Noi grew up without a single friend. As Noi grew older, her anger, loneliness, and sense of worthlessness grew too.

Feeling terrible about the choice she had made, Noi's mother tried her best to support her daughter, freeing her from duties on the farm so she could study. "People respect the wealthy," she told Noi. So with money as the goal and purpose of her life, Noi left her village for the big city of Bangkok. She hoped that studying business at the university and becoming successful would finally stop the insults and silence the inner voice that insisted that her whole life was a pointless mistake.

It wasn't long into her life in Bangkok that Noi felt the familiar loneliness returning. Her sister-in-law, a Buddhist like Noi, had some helpful advice for making new friends: "I've heard that Christians are friendly and welcome newcomers." It sounded like good advice. Noi didn't know any Christians or where to find them, but she remembered their affinity for crosses. So as Noi walked the city streets, she looked for buildings with crosses on them. To her delight, she found one right beside her campus.

Noi began to attend church, but she wasn't looking for God. She just wanted friends. At church Noi not only found the friendship she craved but also discovered a depth of community and purpose she hadn't known. Her new friends gave her a Bible written in both Thai and English, which Noi thought would be perfect to help her learn English. So she started reading . . . and reading and reading. As she read the Bible, she encountered God and learned that a relationship with God was what her heart had been hungering for all along. This relationship changed Noi's life by changing the way she saw herself and others. Ironically, Noi's perspective of herself began to change not through positive self-talk or nurturing her self-esteem like Western culture so often prescribes but rather by taking the focus off of herself and placing it on the God who created and loved her.

After university, Noi went into business and soon became fixated on the rat race of success. She was so busy making money that she didn't have time for her family. Then one day, her father died. This was a pivotal moment in Noi's life. She realized that the way she saw herself had changed, but that the truth of Jesus hadn't changed the way she lived or affected the decisions she was making. She felt a huge burden when she realized that she hadn't even made the time to tell her father about Jesus and how he was changing her life. Noi went to her pastor and asked a life-changing question: "What is important to God? What does God want me to do with my life?" Her pastor explained, "The heart of God is to see people come into healthy community with him and people." She was struck by the fact that God is the one who gives life purpose, and she wanted to share his transformational love.

Initially, this proved to be easier said than done. Noi was still so hurt from the way people had treated her that she found it difficult at first to love people. But as she spent time reading the Bible, praying, and working alongside other men and women who loved God, her heart changed and she slowly learned to care for people. One day, she saw an elderly woman sitting under a nearby tree. Throughout the day, Noi noticed that this woman sat there for hours and not once did someone come talk with her. Noi's heart broke for her and she wondered what this lady was thinking about all that time. Her body was there, but where did her mind go? Was she thinking about her youth? Did she have a husband and children? What kind of community did she have? Or was she always alone?

This was a life-changing moment for Noi. As she took her attention off of herself and placed it on God, God brought the humanity of others into focus. The thought of this woman just wouldn't leave Noi alone, and soon she found herself looking into the condition of the elderly in Bangkok. Noi decided to use her skills in business to start a nonprofit ministry to help care for the elderly. Like a good businesswoman, she researched the situation thoroughly, even going so far as to live as a resident in a nursing home for ten days to learn what could be improved. She told me that on her first day in the nursing home she met a man who told her that he felt like a bird. Noi asked him, "Why do you feel like a bird?" He responded, "Because I sit here in my cage waiting to be fed at breakfast, waiting to be fed at lunch, waiting to be fed at dinner. That's my life in this cage, waiting." He confessed to her, "I just want to die." Noi began to cry.

Noi realized that it's easy to treat a human being as something less than human, as just a body that needs to be fed and cleaned. Her own life had taught her that people need much more than that. People need to be loved, they need relationships, and they need meaning and purpose. This man wanted to die because he had been stripped of his humanity. Eventually, Noi started the Ruth Center, an incredible nonprofit organization dedicated to loving and supporting the elderly alongside their children as they care for their aging parents.

WHAT IS A HUMAN?

In the previous chapter we saw the evil that people are capable of when they lose sight of their humanity and the humanity of others. Dehumanization leads to suffering. Noi understood that all too clearly as she struggled to find herself amid the pain of people's abusive actions and words. However, as you can see with Noi's story, the opposite is also true. Humanization leads to compassion. As a parent, I am continually reminded that this is one of my greatest responsibilities—to teach my children a correct view of themselves that leads to compassion for others. This is a challenging task given the state of our culture. No longer do you need a physical abnormality, such as Noi's, to attract the scorn of peers. Polarizing political, religious, philosophical, social, and scientific views have made it increasingly easy to demean and mistreat each other with our language and with our actions, especially online. Harassment and violence will continue to be a regular part of life in the twenty-first century if we do not see each other's humanity correctly. But how do we humanize? What does it mean to be human?

So many people today do not have a clear idea of what a human is. We live in a culture that confuses what a thing is with what it is made of. I was reminded of this one day when I took my kids to the public library. Ever since my boys Tristan and William were little, my wife and I have worked hard to inspire in them a love for reading and thinking. This has meant many trips to the library to get books. Their favorites have often been about outer space and how everything works.

While looking at books about our solar system, my son picked up a children's picture book titled *You Are Stardust* and we sat down to read it together.[1] Amid beautiful illustrations of plants and animals, the author clearly articulates the commonly held view that people are nothing more than cosmic dust. The author explains that people are made of carbon and carbon is made from dying stars. Therefore, as Carl Sagan famously concluded, "we are made of star stuff." Now, that's true— people's bodies are made of carbon. But is that it? Are we just cosmic waste adrift in the universe, or are we something more?

SCIENCE KILLED THE SCIENTIST

The idea of reducing a thing to what it is made of is not new but goes back, like many things, to the Greeks. Leucippus and Democritus were philosophers in the fifth century BC, and they believed that everything, from volcanoes to elephants to houses, is made of matter and thus theoretically could be divided into smaller and smaller parts. Logic also dictates that a moment must occur when matter is no longer divisible. At some point you get to the smallest bit of stuff. This is where the word *atom* originates. It means "uncuttable." Atomists believed that everything is made of these uncuttable parts, or atoms, piled together, with empty space or void between them. Democritus expressed this idea plainly: "By convention sweet is sweet, by convention bitter is bitter, by convention hot is hot, by convention cold is cold, by convention color is color. But in reality there are atoms and the void."[2] This formulation of the theory of atomism was the genesis of the first recorded purely physical worldview in which the parts of the universe, the atoms and the void, make up all of reality.

After Leucippus and Democritus, this purely physical view of the world lost popularity for thousands of years, only to be revived again during the Enlightenment. Defining people by what they are made of has continued to grow in popularity over the last couple of centuries. As scientists have investigated the complexities of the universe, it has become necessary to reduce unimaginably huge things, like the universe, to smaller, simpler parts in order to understand their mechanics. It's like when you were a kid and you took apart the toaster to see how it worked. Well, at least I did, and it nearly drove my mother mad, since nothing goes back together as easily as it comes apart! In the same way, people began to take the universe apart bit by bit in order to see how it works. The problem is that in the process, the universe and everything in it came to be viewed as a machine of purely physical parts, operating according to purely physical laws. The cosmos became a clockwork universe.

Nietzsche, a nineteenth-century philosopher, recognized that this mechanical universe meant the death of God. He didn't mean that people had killed God; rather he meant that God was no longer seen as necessary for understanding the universe or as important in people's lives. Even more than that, God was no longer even a possibility because a clockwork universe is closed off to anything nonphysical. Accordingly, people are viewed as small machines within the larger machine of the universe. Humanity is purely physical, just collections of carbon, nitrogen, oxygen, and other atoms organized by DNA, which itself is just more groups of atoms.

Michael Polanyi, a concerned twentieth-century scientist-turned-philosopher, picked up where Nietzsche left off and recognized that this commitment to a purely physical universe meant the death of humanity. It wasn't just God who had died within this worldview; it was people as well. You could say that science, in reducing the world to only its physical parts, had killed the scientist. Polanyi explained that if our science is "unable to recognize any persons, [it] presents us with a picture of the universe in which we ourselves are absent."[3]

The irony of the information age is that humanity's desire to gain information and understand the cosmos has led us to doubt our own existence by seeing ourselves as nothing more than stardust. Within a purely physical view of the universe, there is no way to account for the persons who are doing science, no way to explain the curiosity, freedom, passion, purpose, and trust in our senses which science requires as foundational. Oddly, the parts of the universe have become more real to us than the persons observing those parts.

THE WALKING DEAD

This idea that a merely physical worldview eliminates personhood was clearly illustrated by William Seabrook, the man responsible for unintentionally igniting the zombie craze of the twentieth and twenty-first centuries. Seabrook was an adventurer and a journalist, known today for his bizarre obsessions with occultism, cannibalism, and voodoo. In 1929, he traveled to Haiti to document voodoo and published his experience in *The Magic Island*. During his travels, his guide, Polynice, described a phenomenon called "zombies": sugarcane workers he described as "dead bodies walking, without souls or minds." Seabrook demanded that Polynice take him at once to see these walking dead. This is what he records about his experience upon arriving at the fields:

My first impression of the three supposed *zombies,* who continued dumbly at work, was that there was something about them unnatural and strange. They were plodding like brutes, like automatons . . . The eyes were the worst. It was not my imagination. They were in truth like the eyes of a dead man, not blind, but staring, unfocused, unseeing. The whole face, for that matter, was bad enough. It was vacant, as if there was nothing behind it. It seemed not only expressionless, but incapable of expression. I had seen so much previously in Haiti that was outside ordinary normal experience that for the flash of a second I had a sickening, almost panicky lapse in which I thought, or rather felt, "Great God, maybe this stuff is really true, and if it is true, it is rather awful, for it upsets everything." By "everything" I meant the natural fixed laws and processes on which all modern human thought and actions are based.[4]

Polynice responded with confusion to Seabrook's unwillingness to believe or even to entertain the possibility of a zombie. Seabrook explained his position, saying, "But it is a fixed rule of reasoning in America that we will never accept the possibility of a thing's being 'supernatural' so long as any natural explanation, even farfetched, seems adequate."

Although Seabrook ultimately concluded that zombies aren't real, this small section in his book inspired the very first zombie movie, *White Zombie,* in 1932. But I think there is something even more ironic taking place here. A zombie, by definition, is a purely physical body lacking a soul or a mind. Yet Seabrook refuses to believe in a zombie because it's "supernatural." He has equated the existence of the soul and mind with what is "natural," and classified the body devoid of soul or mind as supernatural. However, in the same breath, Seabrook clings to a worldview which claims that human beings are only physical bodies and that the mind or soul is a delusion since it doesn't physically exist and doesn't follow physical laws. If you follow Seabrook's logic, not only must he conclude that zombies exist, but also he must admit that he is one!

According to Seabrook's physicalism, what is natural is anything that is physical and follows physical laws, and the supernatural is that which is not physical and does not follow physical laws. The problem is that all of the things that we cherish most, and that are essential attributes of our humanity, such as the mind, meaning, purpose, value, love, and justice, are not physical and do not follow physical laws. These things cannot be touched, seen, tasted, or heard, yet every person either intuitively believes that they exist or, at the very least, behaves as though they exist. The mind is not physical, yet, like Seabrook, we are convinced we have one. Love is not physical, and yet anyone who has fallen in love or has children knows that it is real. Meaning is not physical, and yet even the most ardent physicalist admits that it is necessary to behave as though it exists.

PLAYING PRETEND

One such physicalist is Yuval Noah Harari. He is the author of the popular book *Sapiens,* in which he relies on evolutionary biology to define humanity, explain human history, and predict the future of humanity, all without God. In the book, he vehemently affirms the physicalist position that nonphysical things like meaning cannot exist. He says, "As far as we can tell, from a purely scientific viewpoint, human life has absolutely no meaning. Humans are the outcome of blind evolutionary processes that operate without goal or purpose. Our actions are not part of some divine cosmic plan, and if planet Earth were to

blow up tomorrow morning, the universe would probably keep
going about its business as usual . . . Hence *any* meaning that
people ascribe to their lives is just a delusion."[5]

With this as his starting place, you would think that he
would deny any meaning in his own life or at least live his life
consistently as if meaning isn't real. Yet he admits that although
meaning is a delusion, it is a delusion that is crucial for happiness and normal behavior in humans. He says, "A meaningful
life can be extremely satisfying even in the midst of hardship,
whereas a meaningless life is a terrible ordeal no matter how
comfortable it is." Harari writes that in order to be happy,
and for the good of society, we have to convince ourselves that
our lives have meaning, even though we know the truth to
be otherwise, and then he admits, "This is quite a depressing
conclusion."

Do you see the absurd leaps that the physicalist must make
in order to explain away what we all know to be true? When we
deny nonphysical realities, we are required to reject the existence
of meaning and purpose for humanity, yet at the same time,
humanity seems to require the existence of nonphysical realities
like meaning and purpose. Harari's answer to this dilemma is
just to embrace the cognitive dissonance. We should just accept
that what we know to *be* objectively true and what is essential
for us to *believe* to be true are diametrically opposed.

Harari applies the same principle to other nonphysical realities such as human equality and human rights, which he, like
a good physicalist, also claims do not exist. He writes, "We
believe in a particular order not because it is objectively true,
but because believing in it enables us to cooperate effectively
and forge a better society."[6] Human rights don't exist, but it is
better for us to pretend that they do.

I don't know about you, but that answer is not satisfying.
I don't want to just stick my head in the sand and accept that

how I act must be different from what I know. Most of all, these mental gymnastics are unnecessary. It's much simpler to go back to the origins of the clockwork universe and admit that its premise is flawed. If we acknowledge that the physical world is not all there is, that human beings are more than just the physical parts our bodies are made of, suddenly everything falls into place and the cognitive dissonance disappears.

Physical and nonphysical realities work together beautifully to explain all of life. They are connected in the same way that pure science (like physics) and applied science (like engineering) work together. Physics is concerned with *gaining information* about the physical parts of the universe and the laws that they follow. These laws are absolute and never fail. For example, oxygen always switches from a liquid to a gas at minus 182.95°C. Engineering, on the other hand, is concerned with *using that information* to arrange those physical parts to achieve a particular purpose. Unlike with physics, engineered objects *can* fail to follow the purposes for which they were designed. NASA engineers used their knowledge of the physical properties of oxygen, including its boiling point, to design a liquid oxygen tank for the purpose of supplying astronauts with air, water, and electricity. When that liquid oxygen tank exploded fifty-six hours into the flight of *Apollo 13*, the laws of physics were never violated, but the laws of human engineering sure were! That tank failed to fulfill its engineered purpose, with near disastrous results.

The difference between physics and engineering is similar to the difference between physical and nonphysical realities. Science is used to study the parts that something is made of and describe how those parts interact. Religion, however, is interested in the purpose something was created for. If you want to know the meaning of something, the purpose for which a thing was made, that's a question only its creator can answer.

THE HUMANITY OF LEGO

If we are to understand human beings as more than just physical parts that follow physical laws, we need to understand the purpose for which we were created. This is so intuitive to us that we do it naturally. We always define a created thing according to its purpose and not its parts. For example, if you ask me what that little machine on my wrist is, I would not define it as an interesting combination of glass, metal, and leather. I would tell you it's a watch! Why? Because something that has been created or engineered is always defined by its purpose, not its parts.

The same is true of the Lego that my children love to play with. They understand the difference between a bag of plastic parts and the purposeful arrangement of those parts into a rocket ship. Sometimes my children get extra creative with their Lego and it's hard for me to tell whether that elaborate gadget on the living room floor is a vehicle, a monster, or something else. In cases like that, I don't decide to invent my own meaning or purpose for it. Instead, I need to go to the creator, my son, and ask him.

Just like with Lego, there is a difference between a universe full of stardust and the purposeful arrangement of that dust into a human being. If we want to know what a human is, we need to know not only what we are made of but also the purpose we were created for. Because people did not bring themselves into existence, this is not a question we can answer by ourselves. This is a theological question, a question for the architect, the engineer, the creator of the universe.

PURPOSEFULLY CREATED

The Bible offers a worldview that makes sense of our experience. Genesis 1:1 says, "In the beginning God created the heavens and the earth." The Hebrew word for "create" means to bring something new and unique into existence. The universe began to exist as a creative act of God. It's important to understand that God is not some kind of mechanical unseen force like gravity. God is a person. God has a will and he chose to create.

Notice that the act of creation is always an act of purpose, and an act of purpose is an act of creation. You can't separate the two. They are two sides of the same coin. I was once challenged on this point by a graduate student. She was an artist, and she asked, "Andy, what if I were to create a painting with no purpose?" Her question reminded me that sometimes the obvious answers can be the hardest to see. I kindly responded to her that *that* would be the purpose of the painting—to have no purpose. It would be the reason why she created it. It's one of those truths you can't escape. An act of creation is always an act of purpose.

Genesis 2 explains that God took the dust of the cosmos, the atoms and the void, and breathed life into them, purposefully fashioning those parts into a whole person, a human being. The message of the Bible from beginning to end is that God created humanity for the purpose of relationship. Jesus consistently taught that God loves us and desires that we love him and people.

In Mark 12, Jesus was asked, "What's the greatest commandment?" This was the Jewish equivalent of asking, "What is the meaning or purpose of life?" Jesus answered, "'Love the Lord your God with all your heart and with all your soul and with all your mind and with all your strength.' The second is this: 'Love your neighbor as yourself.' There is no commandment greater than these."[7]

The Bible explains that this is the purpose of life and what it means to be human: to love God and love people. You'll remember that this is the same message that Noi's pastor told her when she was searching for purpose in her life. God created humanity to love and be loved, to know and be known. A human being is that which has been made with the purpose of having a loving relationship with God and people. We were created for community.

The Bible, then, is not a book about the parts that a person is made of but a book about the purpose we were made for. It is a message from the one who created us and wants to see our purpose brought to completion. The Bible is the guide to our humanity. God alone can define us, give our lives value, and show us what will lead to our flourishing. It's when we lose sight of God that our humanity becomes distorted and we dehumanize ourselves and others. This is what makes Jesus' life so compelling. He loved God and people. It's also what makes his teaching so powerful. He challenged people to have a correct view of God and each other.

A HUMANIZING TWIST

One of the most effective ways that Jesus corrected our perspective was with the use of story. In the gospel of Luke, chapter 10, a religious man asks Jesus this question: "What must I do to inherit eternal life?"[8] Jesus replies, "What is written in the Law?" The man replies by quoting what he has, most likely, already heard Jesus teach: "'Love the Lord your God with all your heart and with all your soul and with all your strength and with all your mind'; and, 'Love your neighbor as yourself.'" Jesus affirms that he has answered correctly. But the man isn't finished. He then asks the real question he is wrestling with: "Who is my neighbor?" In other words, "Who do I have to love?"

Jesus answers this question with the now-famous story of the good Samaritan. It's helpful to understand that in the first century, Samaritans were called "half-breeds" because they did not have a pure Jewish bloodline. As well, they held different religious beliefs than the Jews. Thus, they were viewed as lesser humans, unfit to talk to, eat with, or marry. Jews even went out of their way to avoid walking through Samaritan land. The Samaritans were not viewed as neighbors or even as fully human and deserving of love. They were a convenient exception to God's purpose, and this man wants justification for his dehumanizing actions.

So Jesus tells him a story in which a Jew lying on the road, beaten and robbed, is helped by a low-class Samaritan after even the most esteemed Jewish religious leaders do not come to his aid. It's a story with a humanizing twist. Have you ever noticed how most movies humanize the hero and dehumanize the villain? That's the familiar narrative, especially when you're seeking to justify your bias toward a person or group of people. Unexpectedly, Jesus takes the commonly dehumanized enemy of the Jews, a Samaritan, and humanizes him into the hero in order to change this man's perspective. In the story, the Samaritan does for the Jew what the Jew doesn't want to do for the Samaritan—see him as a fellow human being.

It's convicting to ponder: if you asked Jesus the same question—Who is my neighbor?—who would Jesus make the hero of the story? Who are the people today that we seek justification for not seeing as fully human and deserving of our love? If we're honest, many of us are tempted to justify dehumanizing those people we dislike or disagree with. It's interesting to note that Jesus disagreed with the Samaritans' religious beliefs. Yet Jesus walked through their lands, ate with them, talked with them, healed them, and offered the same salvation to them. Jesus understood that loving people and disagreeing with them are not mutually exclusive. You can do both, and he proved it. Sometimes disagreeing with people is one of the most loving things you can do.

Interestingly, this reversal of hero and villain is a theme in many of Charles Dickens' stories. Meant for more than just entertainment, his novels challenged the warped Victorian worldview that dehumanized people according to the caste system of the aristocracy. One of my favorites is *Oliver Twist,* a story about a lowly orphan who is treated like garbage until one day a stunning twist of fate reveals him to be the lost heir to a family fortune. It's not just a rags-to-riches story but a subhuman-to-human story. The "villain" becomes the hero. Through his stylish prose, Dickens lures his readers into a philosophical conundrum: What changed? Oliver didn't change, so why has everyone's perspective of him so drastically reversed? For Dickens, this was more than a story. It was personal. His father had served time in a debtors' prison and his family had been the object of subhuman scorn. His family knew well what it felt like to be viewed as less than human.

The twist in *Oliver Twist* is similar to what happened in Noi's life. As with Oliver, the circumstances of Noi's birth ensured that others saw her as worthless. Noi initially chased money, thinking that it would solve her problems. Instead, Noi found something much greater. She encountered God and reclaimed her humanity. In Jesus she found a wealth of purpose, and by following his example, she learned how to love and humanize all people.

Remember how the elderly Thai man compared his life to that of a caged bird? The lack of love and attention from others felt dehumanizing to him. The reality is that in a world without God, we all become like caged birds as well: mouths to feed, bodies to take care of, but without any purpose in life. Jesus reclaims our humanity with the truth that we are much more than atoms, that we were made for a purpose.

PART 2

WHAT IS THE VALUE
OF HUMAN LIFE?

FURBABIES

While living in Southern California, I often took my kids to the park to play. My two young boys enjoyed the chance to run around unhindered, and I, after a decade of living in Canada, enjoyed soaking up the warm California sun. One day at the playground, I noticed a man pushing a baby stroller. He strolled along the grass toward the swing set, talking to what I assumed was his baby. To my surprise, once he got closer to me I saw that there wasn't a child inside but a dog. Well, truthfully, I wasn't that surprised. During my time on the West Coast I had come to see some pretty strange things. Yet what he did next was bizarre, even by Cali standards. Stopping the stroller beside the swings, the man picked up his tiny sweater-vested terrier and placed it in the children's swing. My kids and I couldn't help but stare as the man gently pushed his dog, cheering as it went higher and higher. I'll never forget the look on that dog's face! It was a look of puzzled concern, similar to my own, I'm sure.

We've all seen those people who take their animal relationships a little too far, haven't we? Now, don't get me wrong— our family has a Labradoodle named Wilson and we love him. We take him paddleboarding, dress him up for Halloween (he makes a great Darth Vader), and have taught him some pretty great tricks. I know we're not the only ones. Many people love

their pets, and humankind has a long, rich history of relationships with animals. Yet things have certainly changed in the
past decade. We are living in a culture in which one in six pets
has its own social media account. One Pomeranian named Jiff
has almost nine million followers. In a 2018 survey of dog owners, 31 percent claimed that their dog is the little spoon when
they sleep and 19 percent said their dog is the big spoon—a
fact I really didn't need to know![1] A similar survey showed that
65 percent of millennials would find it more stressful to be separated from their pets for a week than from their cell phones and
that 70 percent would be willing to take a pay cut if it meant
that they could bring their pets to work.[2] Recently, "more space
for a dog" ranked as the third highest motivator for people
purchasing a home, eclipsing both marriage and children in
importance.

We could spend a whole day online perusing the silly items
that people buy for their pets—I've even bought some of them
myself. But while it's easy to lightheartedly tease a man who
pushes his dog on the swing, it's more difficult to really wrestle
with the philosophical ideas underlying this pet-soaked culture.
Our world is deeply confused about what it means to be a person with value.

We all understand that people are valuable. That's never
really been contested. However, the origin of that idea *is* highly
debated, because at root, it is profoundly Christian: God made
all creatures, but he created humans uniquely in his image
and bestowed value on them. But in a world without God,
where *does* human value come from and who does it apply
to? Are animals people? We may call them "furbabies" and
even "furgrandbabies," but should we value them like human
children? This raises significant questions: Are human beings
more valuable than animals? Are they the same as animals? Or,
at times, might they even be less valuable?

AARDVARKS AND LETTUCES

When we remove God from the creation of life in general and of human life in particular, we must find some other explanation to account for where life comes from. In the West, the usual story to replace God is some form of evolutionary biology: humans have evolved just like the other animals, and all of our abilities and desires—for love, justice, cooperation, morality—don't come from a purposeful, objective foundation but instead arise from genes that nature has selected for us. If that is the case, then when it comes down to the idea of human value and human rights, we can't claim that value and rights are universal and inalienable. As Yuval Noah Harari puts it, "According to the science of biology, people were not 'created.' They have evolved. And they certainly did not evolve to be 'equal.' The idea of equality is inextricably intertwined with the idea of creation. The Americans got the idea of equality from Christianity . . . Just as people were never created, neither, according to the science of biology, is there a 'Creator' who 'endows' them with anything. There is only a blind evolutionary process, devoid of any purpose, leading to the birth of individuals."[3]

So if human value can't be rooted in something inherent to human beings naturally, then how do we answer the question of whether humans are valuable compared with animals?

One position holds that because humans are essentially the same as animals biologically, they have exactly the same value as them. Ingrid Newkirk, the founder of PETA (People for the Ethical Treatment of Animals), famously captured the essence of this argument by saying, "A rat is a pig is a dog is a boy."[4] To show how seriously they believe this, in 2003 PETA organized a pro-vegetarian campaign called Holocaust on Your Plate.[5] As the name implies, the traveling exhibit compared modern farming practices to the Nazi genocide of the Jews. Giant billboards displayed photographs of piles of Jewish corpses beside photographs of piles of dead pigs. Another one compared images of bunk beds in a concentration camp to chickens in tiered cages. Killing animals for food, they argued, is equivalent to killing people. Both should be valued exactly the same way.

Influential ethicist Peter Singer holds a second position. He agrees with Newkirk that humans are fundamentally the same as animals and rejects that humans are inherently valuable because they are human. Instead, he claims that we must rely on a range of characteristics, such as the capacity to feel pain or pleasure, as well as certain thresholds of intellectual or emotional ability, in order to bestow value onto creatures. On that basis, then, in certain circumstances, animals have more value than humans. He writes,

> We may legitimately hold that there are some features of certain beings which make their lives more valuable than those of other beings; but there will surely be some non-human animals whose lives, by any standards, are more valuable than the lives of some humans. A chimpanzee, dog, or pig, for instance, will have a higher degree of self-awareness and a greater capacity for meaningful relations with others than a severely retarded infant or someone in a state of advanced senility. So if we base the right to life on these characteristics we must grant these animals a right to life as good as, or better than, such retarded or senile humans . . . This is why when we consider members of our own species who lack the characteristics of normal humans we can no longer say that their lives are always to be preferred to those of other animals.[6]

Singer famously argues that to value an animal below a human is speciesism—the belief that one's own species is superior to another—which he claims is a moral evil comparable to racism or sexism.

To be fair, both Newkirk and Singer clearly love and respect animals and want them to be treated ethically. This is a right and noble aim, one that I wholeheartedly agree with. The problem lies in their method. Both of these positions attempt to raise the value of animals by humanizing them, hoping that placing human value onto an animal will eventually lead people to take better care of them.

This hope was clearly articulated at a 2018 conference that I helped organize around the question, "What is the foundation for human rights?" Andy Bannister, a Christian, represented the traditional sanctity of human life position, arguing that human value and therefore basic human rights are rooted in God as the creator of life. Justin Trottier represented a secular humanist position, arguing that it is possible for human rights to exist in a world without God. At one point in the discussion, the question of human dignity came up, and specifically who qualifies for that dignity. Andy questioned the idea that the value of a creature should be based on its capacities or abilities, bringing up a dehumanizing trend taking place in Scandinavian countries toward people with Down syndrome. Ultimately, he argued, atheism has a real problem with not knowing where to draw the boundaries of who is valued and who is not. He explained, "The problem with going down the capacity route is if you draw those capacities too tightly, then you do start excluding vast numbers of the human community, the very very young, the very very old, those who are profoundly disabled. And if you draw them too loosely, then you do start drawing in all other kinds of things . . . you start drawing in all kinds of life: rats and aardvarks and lettuces and so on and so forth."[7]

Justin responded:

It *is* a real problem. But that's why my reaction to that problem is to go the other route. Not to dehumanize— those are horrifying stories that you're talking about, dehumanizing people with Down syndrome—but to humanize more non-humans perhaps. And not just chimpanzees, or other animals. What if we encounter alien intelligence? It might sound kind of speculative, but: those are not humans, but they're persons, in a philosophical sense. Should we not be expanding protection and, of course, the same kind of rights to them? What about where we're going with artificial intelligence? . . . I would rather actually go the other route and humanize more things, than fall into this trap of potentially going the other way and dehumanizing.

What Justin was proposing is something I am hearing more and more often. Because people respect human value, it appears logical to give that value to more things such as animals, machines, and even aliens. In fact, this granting of human value to other things has been taking place all over the world. A river was granted personhood in New Zealand, a gorilla was granted humanity in Spain, and a robot named Sophia was given citizenship in Saudi Arabia. This is a growing trend, and it's extremely dangerous. Instead of raising the value of rivers, robots, and gorillas, it's doing the opposite. It is diluting the value of humanity.

Let's consider the case of Sophia the robot. In this age of artificial intelligence, it is often argued that a machine that can convincingly mimic humanity should be considered human. However, remember that created things are defined by their purpose. They can either succeed at fulfilling that purpose or not, but what they can't do is change what they are. Just because an airplane is good at flying doesn't mean that we should consider it a bird. The best human-mimicking robot in the world is still just that—a human-imitating machine.

Consider that when human value is opened up to other things, it is no longer inherent but is now something that we decide on. Herein lies the problem. Who gets to decide what qualifies for human value? As soon as value can be earned, it can also be taken away. This is the challenge with granting humanity based on ability: who gets to decide what qualifies? There is a big difference between imitating an infant and imitating an adult. If we designed a "human test" that every machine has to pass to be considered human, what would happen to those humans who fail? Couldn't we imagine a computer passing the test while a small child fails? Would that child no longer be considered human? Consider that Peter Singer was basically arguing that the same test should be employed with animals. Those animals that are more human-like, such as gorillas, would pass the test, while certain humans, such as babies and the disabled, would fail.

This is more than just theoretical. Historically, we have drawn the boundaries for what qualifies as human in all sorts of different places. The results have been horrifying. Anytime animals have been equated with humans, the result has always been a lowering of human value and the exclusion of some people from the human race. When humans get to draw the boundaries of value, they will always include some and exclude others.

THE HEART OF DARKNESS

One day when I was in Belgium, I was reminded of this dehumanizing effect of equating humans with animals. I had decided to take a quick trip into Brussels to see a controversial statue. The minute I arrived, I was reminded of the tension surrounding this landmark. I had just pulled out my phone to take a picture when a concerned Belgian woman in her midthirties asked, "Do you know who that is?" She wanted to make absolutely sure that I understood who I was taking a picture of. It was clear from her tone that she was not proud of the image. I looked again at the giant horse and rider. The man sat astride the horse with his chest puffed out and his head held high as if he were ready to defend his actions to the nation and the world. Within the past few years, Belgians had defaced the statue a number of times by smearing it with red paint and campaigned to have the statue removed. I looked a little closer. Large letters at the base of the statue read "Leopold II." Below that was inscribed the date of his reign, 1865–1909, as well as the words *Patria Memor,* a call for the homeland to remember.

That call to remember is understandably haunting for many Belgians because Leopold's reign was not a moment of triumph but rather one of the darkest chapters in human history. In 1865, at the age of thirty, Leopold II succeeded his father as the king of Belgium. More than a ruler, King Leopold was an entrepreneur. He desired wealth and power and decided that colonization was the quickest route to both. After a number of failed attempts to purchase a colony for himself, Leopold set out in a private venture to cut his own piece of what he called the "magnificent African cake."[8] He sent explorer Henry Stanley to what was commonly known then as the "dark continent" to lay claim to the Congo. In 1885, Leopold was granted private ownership of the Congo Free State. It was an ironic name given that he immediately enslaved the people and plundered the land of its natural resources. The Congolese slaves were forced into prostitution and labor in the rubber fields. They also helped harvest elephants by the thousands for the ivory trade.

Leopold's Congo set the stage for Joseph Conrad's famous novella *Heart of Darkness.* Conrad had been a steamboat captain on the Congo River and had a front-row seat to the barbarism of Leopold's African enterprise. Some of Conrad's characters were even based on real people and real experiences. Author Adam Hochschild suggests that the character of Mr. Kurtz was based on Leon Rom, because both Mr. Kurtz and Rom enjoyed writing, painting, and collecting human heads.[9] Rom's home in the Congo used twenty-one human heads as garden decorations.

With people like Rom in charge of the Congo, it's not surprising to learn that the conditions of the labor camps were horrific. Whole tribes were wiped out by violence and disease. They were beaten, tortured, mutilated, raped, and murdered. The photographs that survived those atrocities testify to the horrors that the people went through. Congolese men, women, and children had their hands, feet, and noses cut off as punishment. One of the more gut-wrenching pictures of dehumanization captures a father being forced to stare at the severed hand and foot of his child because he hadn't worked hard enough in the rubber fields. Sadly, in only twenty-three years, more than half of the Congolese population was wiped out. It is generally agreed upon that Leopold was responsible for the death of some ten million Congolese, a death toll on par with the Holocaust.

It's no wonder that the statue of Leopold II in Brussels is so controversial. That day as I stared at it, I pondered once again how an individual could be capable of such wickedness. Did he not value human life? Well, just like every oppressor before and after him, the truth is that he *did* value human life. If you could go back in time and ask Leopold and those working for him, even people such as Rom, whether enslaving, mutilating, and killing people is wrong, they would have answered, "Yes, of course it's wrong!" But, they would have explained, the Congolese are not humans. They are animals.

HUMAN ZOO

The belief that sub-Saharan Africans were basically animals was widely held at the time of Leopold II. Given the wealth to be found on the African continent, this was a convenient worldview that allowed for widespread exploitation. However, this view wasn't just motivated by dollars and cents. It also was supported by science. According to the science being taught at that time in the nation's top universities, black Africans were less evolved than white Europeans, somewhere between an ape and a human on the evolutionary timeline.

This idea was dramatically demonstrated in 1906 when a pygmy man from the Congo named Ota Benga was put on display in the monkey house at the Bronx Zoo in New York City. He shared a cage with an orangutan. Thousands of people came to the zoo to see this supposed missing link in the evolutionary chain. It wasn't until an influential pastor by the name of Robert MacArthur visited the zoo that things began to change. He spoke out against the injustice and helped organize the city's African-American clergy to protest the exhibit. The group of clergy was led by Rev. James Gordon, who expressed their grievance, saying, "Our race, we think, is depressed enough, without exhibiting one of us with apes. We think we are worthy of being considered human beings, with souls."[10] They were successful in freeing Ota Benga, but a few years later, after he attempted unsuccessfully to return to the Congo because of the outbreak of World War I, Ota Benga shot himself in the heart.

THE "LOGIC" OF SLAVERY

The idea that some humans are lower and more animalistic than others did not begin with Leopold II in the Congo. Ancient Greek philosopher Aristotle expressed similar beliefs more than two thousand years earlier. Aristotle's views had a lot in common with later theories about capacity because he relied on the characteristics of people in order to determine their value. He set the stage for slavery throughout the centuries by arguing that it is natural. He reasoned that some people are strong and some are weak. Some people are intelligent and others are not. People are not naturally equal in their appearance or abilities. Therefore, Aristotle concluded, some people are superior to others. Natural slaves, he believed, are not fully human because their ability to reason is not sufficient for them to rule themselves. Aristotle concluded that slaves forfeit any rights because, like animals, they require a competent master to direct them. He even made the animal comparison directly, writing that the ox is a "poor man's slave."[11]

Aristotle argued that this hierarchy of slaves and their masters was an inarguable fact of life. He said, "Both master and slave are designed by nature for their positions." This statement about "nature's caste system" eventually received its scientific justification two thousand years later, in 1835, when Charles Darwin first arrived in the Galapagos Islands and began to develop the idea that we now know as the survival of the fittest. His book *On the Origin of Species* is acknowledged today as the cornerstone of evolutionary biology. The great diversity of life, he proposed, came not from a creative God but from naturally occurring variations over long periods of time that led to the evolution of different species. Beneath his main argument lies a more subtle refrain that echoes Aristotle. The oft-forgotten subtitle of Darwin's work best captures it: *By Means of Natural Selection or the Preservation of Favoured Races in the Struggle for Life.* Just as Aristotle thought, the natural world seemed to imply a hierarchy among creatures. In his book *The Descent of Man,* Darwin calls Europeans "the summit of civilisation"[12] and says that they "immeasurably surpass their former savage progenitors."[13] Later on he claims, "At some future period, not very distant as measured by centuries, the civilised races of man will almost certainly exterminate, and replace, the savage races throughout the world."[14]

WELL BORN

Twenty-four years after *On the Origin of Species* was published, Darwin's half-cousin Francis Galton coined the term *eugenics,* from a Greek word meaning "well born," to express his view that some people are more favored or valuable than others. At one time Galton even advocated that the British state intervene in the genetic future of their people. He suggested that if well-born families were willing to arrange genetically advantageous marriages for their children, they should be financially rewarded. In the long run, he reasoned, the gifted offspring that resulted from these marriages would be worth the cost to the government.

Although eugenic ideas didn't gain traction in Britain, they did in the United States. At various times in the twentieth century, eugenics was federally funded in thirty-two states through various programs. Some instituted immigration restrictions on certain races. Others criminalized interracial marriages. Most startling were programs to sterilize "undesirable" people, including immigrants, criminals, Native Americans, people of color, the poor, unmarried mothers, the disabled, and the mentally ill. Even the Supreme Court supported eugenic laws. In the case of *Buck v. Bell,* Supreme Court Justice Oliver Wendell Holmes upheld a forced sterilization law in Virginia, saying, "It is better for all the world, if instead of waiting to execute degenerate offspring for crime, or to let them starve for their imbecility, society can prevent those who are manifestly unfit from continuing their kind.

The principle that sustains compulsory vaccination is broad enough to cover cutting the Fallopian tubes. Three generations of imbeciles are enough."[15]

The ruling in *Buck v. Bell* has never been officially overturned by the Supreme Court.

It's often forgotten that this issue of eugenics is one of the factors that sparked the creation-versus-evolution debate, immortalized forever in the Scopes "Monkey" Trial. Eugenics and evolution were so tied together in the minds of early-twentieth-century Americans that the two words were practically synonymous. This was one reason why Christians were upset that evolution was being taught in schools. Mr. John T. Scopes, a high school teacher, taught from a textbook called *Civic Biology* that justified racism as the natural result of some people's being more evolved than others. The textbook claimed that there are five different races of men and said, "The highest type of all [is] the Caucasians, represented by the civilized white inhabitants of Europe and America."[16]

It shouldn't be surprising that the eugenics ideas developed in the United States eventually inspired and laid the blueprint for Nazi Germany's pursuit of a master race. Adolf Hitler once told a colleague, "I have studied with great interest the laws of several American states concerning prevention of reproduction by people whose progeny would, in all probability, be of no value or be injurious to the racial stock." Only a few years later, this interest turned into action. One of the first laws he passed after gaining control of Germany in 1933 was a compulsory sterilization law under which doctors were required to report to the state all individuals deemed genetically unfit. Around four hundred thousand people were forcibly sterilized by 1939. In 1916, Madison Grant, an American lawyer and zoologist, wrote a well-known book called *The Passing of the Great Race*.[17] Hitler later referred to this book as his Bible, and it was clear that he took its suggestions to heart. He based the creation of Jewish ghettos directly on Grant's instructions.[18]

After the Second World War, when the horrifying details of the Nazis' commitment to the principles of social Darwinism and eugenics came to light, scientists were rightly horrified. It was at this moment, after such a severe failure, that inherent dignity, equality, and human rights were officially cemented into modern society as some of our primary values. It was in response to the fallout of the Holocaust that the UN's Universal Declaration of Human Rights came into being.

SOULLESS SELFIE

Removing God from the creation of human life and substituting him with blind naturalism ultimately undermines inherent human value and leads to a warped perspective of personhood. Suddenly, it becomes a lot less clear what the difference is between animals and humans and what moral obligations apply to each group. As we've seen, confusion about the difference between animals and humans ultimately leads to dehumanization. That confusion is actually one of the reasons why dehumanization is so prevalent in the first place.

I've often looked at photographs of people's evil deeds, such as those committed against the Jews or the Congolese, and thought, "Why would they take a picture? It's psychotic!" Yet the more I've studied this topic, the more I have realized that they took pictures because they weren't ashamed. They were blind to what they were doing because they didn't see those people as whole people. In their eyes, they might as well have been photographing a zoo, a kennel, or a farm.

A similar attitude was revealed in 2004 when CBS broke the story of Abu Ghraib prison. American soldiers stationed in

Iraq had taken pictures of themselves dehumanizing the inmates through torture and mocking them in horrendous scenes. Photographs showed Iraqi prisoners with dog leashes around their necks, their naked bodies being dragged on the concrete. The world was stunned not only by what they saw but also by the soldiers' inability to see the wickedness of their actions. I remember being baffled by their willingness not only to take these images but also to share them, images in which they are smiling and having a grand time.

It was only at the military trial of the Abu Ghraib perpetrators that details surfaced which hinted at the worldview underlying these crimes. One soldier described a horrific scene he witnessed in which prisoners were forced to perform degrading acts with each other. The guards were entertained by their humiliation. He recalled one of the guards calling out, "Look what these animals do when you leave them alone for two seconds."[19]

Do you see the attitude behind those words? It's the belief that these aren't human beings; they are animals, and therefore it doesn't matter what we do to them.

I want to again make it clear that by discussing the perspectives of Leopold II, the Nazis, and the Abu Ghraib guards, I am not excusing them for their actions. They should be held responsible. They *chose* to view those people as less than human. But if these historical incidents teach us anything, it should be to challenge our willingness to embrace dehumanizing ideas. If we insist that animals are the same as humans and have the same value as them, then we also need to open our eyes to the historical reality of how such a perspective has caused us to act in the past. As we've seen, equating an animal with a human doesn't raise the value of an animal; it leads to the dehumanization of people.

THE SCIENCE OF RACISM

We've just been on a whirlwind tour of history. Ideas first expressed by Aristotle found scientific footing in the writings of Charles Darwin and became justification for dehumanizing events in the Belgian Congo, the dehumanization of Ota Benga, and the mass dehumanization of slavery, eugenics, and the acts of Nazi Germany. These are all events that happened a long time ago, so it is all too tempting to shrug it off as ancient history. Many would claim that science has changed its tune, and that nobody really looks at evolution and race through that lens anymore. Right?

Well, it depends on who you ask.

In a world without God, evolutionary biology necessarily becomes the only way to explain our humanity and the only real source of determining human value. Therefore, we must have some way of applying the principles of evolution to humans. Just because doing so isn't politically correct doesn't mean that some aren't willing to face the dilemma of their atheistic beliefs. James Watson is both an atheist and a world-renowned scientist who won the Nobel Prize for discovering the double-helix structure of DNA in 1953. He has written many bestselling books and is lauded for his contributions to science. The discovery of the structure of DNA has even been touted by many as the single most important scientific discovery of the twentieth century. Yet in 2007, Watson received criticism when he told the *Sunday Times* newspaper that he was "inherently gloomy about the prospect of Africa." He said, "[A]ll our social policies are based on the fact that their intelligence is the same as ours—whereas all the testing says not really . . . There is no firm reason to anticipate that the intellectual capacities of peoples geographically separated in their evolution should prove to have evolved identically. Our wanting to reserve equal powers of reason as some universal heritage of humanity will not be enough to make it so."[20]

The backlash was swift and he immediately lost his job, leading him to such financial difficulty that he became the first Nobel laureate ever to sell his medal. Yet in 2019, a documentary called *American Masters: Decoding Watson* was released on PBS in which he was asked whether his views had changed. He replied, "No, not at all, I would like for them to have changed, that there be new knowledge which says that your nurture is much more important than nature. But I haven't seen any knowledge. And there's a difference on the average between blacks and whites on IQ tests. I would say the difference is, it's genetic."[21]

The response to this latest statement by Watson was even more severe than the first. He received universal disdain in the media, and Cold Spring Harbor Laboratory, the highest ranked genetics research lab in the world, immediately stripped him of several honorary titles.

James Watson's comments are untrue. Some of the smartest people I know have black skin. His claims are racist and cruel, and it was good for the media to condemn them. Yet saying his claims are racist is not an excuse for us to ignore them. His statements may not be politically correct, but we still have to deal with the worldview they are rooted in.

James Watson is wildly wrong. Black people are not genetically inferior to white people. My reasons for that conviction stem from my belief in God. As a Christian, I believe that God is responsible for all life including humanity and that we have all been created equally human. I also believe that each individual has different gifts and abilities. Some people really are more intelligent or beautiful or athletic than others. Yet despite our different strengths and weaknesses, all human beings are equally valuable. No group that we construct, whether based on skin color, family lineage, or ability, is in any way superior to another, because our arbitrary judgments do not bestow equality and value—only God does.

Now, the problem is that most people will agree with only half of my argument. In Western culture, everyone wants to believe my conclusion: that human beings are equal in value. That's why the reaction to James Watson's comments was so universal. However, Western culture also wants to vehemently deny my first premise, that God is the one who created us equal and gives us our value. Yet if our value doesn't come from God, where does it come from? The only logical explanation is that it comes from ourselves. Peter Singer suggests that value comes from certain capacities or abilities that we have, such as consciousness or the ability to feel pain and pleasure. James Watson's comments imply that our equality and subsequently our value come from our intelligence. Yet however you define it, the common thread is that, without God, it *is* a choice— equality and value depend on human decisions. And if it's a choice, then it's changeable. Our culture might decide to agree on universal human value today, but what about tomorrow?

The result is that our society embraces a worldview based on naturalism while also denying the logical results of that worldview. We want to borrow the Christian concept of equal human value while rejecting its roots. The result is that our society says one thing, but our actions reveal different convictions. This internal contradiction makes sense of much of what we see in our Western culture today. It explains why our culture, which puts so much emphasis on fighting racism, is also seeing a surge in white supremacy movements. It explains why our culture, which advocates tolerance and open-mindedness, also embraces filter bubbles and social-media tribalism. It explains why we could condemn James Watson in 2007, yet in 2017 one in four survey respondents rated Muslims as only 60 percent as evolved as Americans.[22]

WE'VE CHANGED, WE PROMISE

It's easy to look at the stories of the past—slavery, eugenics, and Nazism—and think that we've changed. What's harder is acknowledging that the same worldview that led to those horrors is being recycled in our culture under different names. Dr. Andrea Morris, an African-American scientist who acted as a consultant for the documentary about James Watson, feels this tension. She said about Watson, "It's not an old story of an old guy with old views. I would like to think that he has the minority view on who can do science and what a scientist should look like. But to me, it feels very current."[23]

In his book *Homo Deus*, Yuval Noah Harari takes a similar position to James Watson, this time in regard to the Nazis' ideas about race. He argues that just because the Nazis took things to an unpleasant extreme doesn't mean that we should throw out the baby with the bathwater. He writes,

[T]he horrors of Nazism should not blind us to whatever insights evolutionary humanism might offer. Nazism was born from the pairing of evolutionary humanism with particular racial theories and ultra-nationalist emotions. Not all evolutionary humanists are racists, and not every belief in humankind's potential for further evolution necessarily calls for setting up police states and concentration camps. Auschwitz should serve as a blood-red warning sign rather than as a black curtain that hides entire sections of the human horizon. Evolutionary humanism played an important part in the shaping of modern culture, and is likely to play an even greater role in the shaping of the twenty-first century.[24]

So while Harari recognizes a problem with the way the Nazis played out their worldview, he is unwilling to say that their basic worldview was wrong. Instead, he suggests that it's possible for our culture to keep the same basic worldview and have a result different from the Holocaust.

I hope that by now that claim rings alarm bells in your head. Despite what we may hope for, both the history of the world and the conditions in our culture prove that when humans get to decide which humans have value, the result is always humanization for some and dehumanization for others.

Later on in his book, Harari explains what he means when he says that evolutionary humanism will have a significant impact on our world in the coming century. He recognizes that in a humanist world—a world where humans decide value instead of God—the basis for universal human value becomes necessarily unstable. As technology changes and evolution continues, the understanding of our humanity and human value will likewise change.

Harari predicts three potential outcomes, none of which are encouraging. First, he says that humans could lose their value completely because all of the capacities and abilities that gave them value in the first place will have been surpassed by technology. Remember, without God, human value can change. Just as horses were replaced by the combustion engine, so humans will be unnecessary and worthless in a world dominated by computers. Second, humans could retain some value as a species, but individuals will lose all of their value because their autonomy will disappear. Algorithms will be so effective that they will run our lives for us and, like Ota Benga a hundred years ago, we will live like caged animals, being fed, watered, and entertained, but lacking any meaningful control over our lives. The third option is even more sinister. He writes, "[S]ome people will remain both indispensable and undecipherable, but they will constitute a small and privileged elite of upgraded humans. These superhumans will enjoy unheard-of abilities and unprecedented creativity, which will allow them to go on making many of the most important decisions in the world . . . However, most humans will not be upgraded, and will consequently become an inferior caste dominated by both computer algorithms and the new superhumans."[25]

Although Harari doesn't use the term, this idea is also known as "transhumanism." It means "beyond human," meaning humans will guide evolution to create a master race. It's a nifty title for an old worldview—eugenics and slavery repackaged for a new generation. Harari may be optimistic about the humanist worldview, but all three of his predictions tell a different story. When humans define value, the result is that we lose value.

There is no doubt that part of Harari's assessment is correct: the twenty-first century will be a time of massive change. It's in such uncertain times that we need to cling to unshakeable truths about who we are and where our value comes from. Humans are not just animals, and seeing them that way will lead only to dehumanization. Our value *is* inalienable, unremovable, and unshakeable, because it is given to us by God.

SHE HAS A HOLE IN HER HEART

In 1999, my sister Lisa received a life-changing phone call. It was only two months before Lisa and her husband, Russ, were to finalize the adoption of their baby girl, Matlynn, from an orphanage in Calcutta, India. Until this moment, everything with the adoption had gone relatively smoothly. Now the orphanage was calling with some bad news and a troubling question. It had come to their attention that Matlynn had been born with some serious health concerns. The doctors knew there was a hole in her heart but suggested that much more could be going on, including the potential for life-altering disabilities. After explaining the situation, the orphanage got to the crux of the matter: "Do you still want her?"

The call went silent as the weight of that question fully landed. It was one of those defining moments when you are forced to come face to face with the hard questions of life. Did a heart defect change the value of this baby girl? What about a disability? Lisa's response broke the silence: "Of course, we still want her!" As she hung up the phone, Lisa and Russ were speechless as the reality of the situation sank in. Yet they were confident that they had made the right decision. Two months later, they welcomed Matlynn into their home and she became part of our family.

Russ and Lisa were determined to love Matlynn despite

health obstacles which proved more challenging than they had initially believed. She spent her first Christmas in the hospital. As the weeks, months, and years went by, they learned that the doctors were right to be worried. Matlynn had much more than a hole in her heart. They learned that Matlynn's birth mother had attempted to abort her. An organization had stepped in to rescue Matlynn after she was born weighing just over two pounds. Although, miraculously, she survived, her mother's choices had left serious wounds. Matlynn has cerebral palsy.

I remember the crushing blow that it was for my sister to learn the depths of her daughter's challenges. Lisa cried for days. She cried not because Matlynn's value was in question. Quite the opposite—she mourned that this priceless child had been devalued and would face so much adversity because of it. Although Lisa and Russ were sad, they didn't give up on Matlynn.

Let's not kid ourselves: life isn't some feel-good movie where problems get resolved in ninety minutes. Matlynn has endured five major surgeries and has the scars to prove it. One surgery cut through both femurs, pulling apart and straightening her legs to help her walk. She has worn leg braces for years, and even now that she's an adult she still needs a cane and falls down regularly—but she gets back up again. The truth is, life is difficult and messy and the challenges we face are lifelong. It can be easy to lose hope.

What about you? In those low moments of your life when you feel worthless, how do you get back up? What's the foundation for your value as a human being?

EMPTY SELF-TALK

This is the question we had to ask as a nation and as a human race after World War II. More human death and devastation took place in the first forty-five years of the twentieth century than the world had ever seen. As we picked ourselves back up from that low point in human history, the question of human value had to be answered. That was the goal of the diverse group of men and women who came together to pen the Universal Declaration of Human Rights (UDHR) in 1948.

The first line of the UDHR reveals the goal of the entire document: "[R]ecognition of the inherent dignity and of the equal and inalienable rights of all members of the human family is the foundation of freedom, justice and peace in the world."[1] That is an incredible declaration! For the first time in history, the countries of the world came together officially and agreed that peace must be built on these three pillars: inherent dignity, equality, and inalienable rights. This document beautifully expresses what we all know to be true of human value.

But there's a hitch.

During the creation of the UDHR, a French philosopher named Jacques Maritain predicted what the central problem with the document would be. He wrote, "[A]t one of the meetings of a Unesco National Commission where Human Rights were being discussed, someone expressed astonishment that certain champions of violently opposed ideologies had agreed on a list of those rights. 'Yes,' they said, 'we agree about the rights, *but on condition that no one asks us why*.'"[2]

The problem, Maritain realized, is that thorny word: why. Although the UDHR captures *what* we all know to be true about human value, it doesn't address *why* we know this to be true. We can fall into the same trap. Our culture embraces the idea of human value but, without God, lacks the foundation, the *why*, to support that belief. It's kind of like when you fall down and use positive self-talk to pick yourself back up again. That might work the first time, but unless you know deep down that those things you tell yourself are actually true, and why, it will become more and more difficult to keep believing. You can play pretend for only so long. In the same way, unless we answer the *why,* assertions of human value just become empty self-talk.

ALL-POWERFUL GOLDEN COW

The first thing the UDHR claims is that humans have inherent dignity. *Dignity* means being worthy of honor and respect, and saying that it is inherent means that it is something we are born with; human beings have value simply on the basis of being human. The UDHR itself is not claiming to give dignity to anyone but is instead simply recognizing it as a preexisting reality.

But in a world without God, is this true? In a naturalistic world, why should we believe that people like Matlynn, you, and me have inherent value? In chapter 3, we saw some of the ways that naturalism tries to answer this question. The best it can offer is that we are no different from animals and that any value we have must stem from some abilities we possess or how evolved we are. There is nothing within naturalism to confirm that human dignity is inherent, other than our just deciding that it is.

Alternatively, the opening chapter of the Bible, Genesis 1, explains that God created everything. He created the universe, the atoms and the void, and he created life itself, from the smallest microorganism to the tallest sequoia. Yet, Genesis tells us, compared with everything else that he created, God made humanity unique. Verses 26–27 say, "Then God said, 'Let us make mankind in our image, in our likeness, so that they may rule over the fish in the sea and the birds in the sky, over the livestock and all the wild animals, and over all the creatures that move along the ground.' So God created mankind in his own image, in the image of God he created them; male and female he created them."

When he made everything else in the cosmos, he did so simply by speaking. But with humans, God did something radically different: "God formed a man from the dust of the ground and breathed into his nostrils the breath of life, and the man became a living being."[3] When he made human beings, God got his hands dirty. He made us in his own image, filled us with his own breath, and then gave us a position of authority over his creation.

This Christian explanation of the world takes the beauty of the UDHR and gives it a backbone, explaining why humanity has inherent dignity. We are all born with value because we were made by God and bear his image. Humanity is a reflection of who God is, and our worth is based in his character and his deeds, not our own. Honor and respect are attributes that must be earned, yet even the smallest baby who hasn't earned anything is worthy of honor and respect because of who God is and what he has done.

I find it significant that the first four commands in the Ten Commandments are all about our view of God. At first glance, it could be easy to assume that God has an identity problem. I mean, why is God so concerned about what we think about him? Yet I've since realized that it isn't God who's having an identity crisis—it's me! God knows that when we lose sight of who he is, we also lose sight of who we are.

I love how a Jewish prayer book puts it: "The gods we worship write their names on our faces, be sure of that. And we will worship something—have no doubt of that either . . . what we are worshipping we are becoming."[4] That statement doesn't mean that we are becoming gods ourselves. Rather, it reminds us that we will always reflect whatever type of god we set our eyes on. If that god is insignificant, then our humanity likewise becomes insignificant. The opposite is also true. If we are made in the image of God, then the greater your view of God, the greater your view of yourself.

You can imagine why God would get so angry in the Bible when people worshiped an idol. In the story of the exodus, the Jews had just escaped from slavery in Egypt and were frustrated as they walked through the wilderness. They lost faith in God and in their leader, Moses, and so they decided to take matters into their own hands by fashioning a calf out of gold and worshiping it.[5] Consider that scene: God has just rescued them from four hundred years of slavery, and instead of following him, they are enslaving themselves to a statue of a cow made out of some melted-down jewelry. If their image of God, the supreme being, was only a cow, then just imagine how they viewed themselves! What about you? We all worship something. What are you worshiping? Money? Fame? Career? Whatever it is, know that it is informing your view of yourself.

THE PRICE IS RIGHT

The UDHR also affirms that all people are equal. Equal, in this case, isn't meant to affirm that we are all born exactly the same or even that we are born with the same opportunities. I once asked Matlynn what she most wished she could do, and she told me she would love to know what it feels like to run and jump. It's easy to forget that we aren't all born with the same bodies, abilities, and circumstances. Instead, when the UDHR uses the word *equal,* it is referring to value and rights. As humans, we all have equal value—no one individual or group is worth more than another—and therefore we should all be treated equally.

Again, we have to ask, in a world without God, is this true? In the last chapter, we saw that a naturalistic view of the world based on evolutionary biology alone doesn't lead us to the conclusion that we are all equally valuable. Instead, the logical conclusions of naturalism provide a pretty compelling philosophical basis for slavery, racism, and other forms of dehumanization. Our culture claims equality as one of its most important tenets, yet when it comes down to it, do we really view all people as equal in value or deserving of equal rights?

Few have struggled with this question more than Kenneth Feinberg. Often called the Master of Disaster, Feinberg is an American attorney who has found a niche specialty in the world of law: divvying up compensation funds to the victims of large disasters. When something terrible happens and a bunch of money comes in to help, Ken is the guy who decides who gets what. He has been appointed to oversee the funds for nearly every major catastrophe of the past few decades, including the September 11 attacks, the Boston Marathon bombings, the Virginia Tech shooting, the Volkswagen emission scandal, and the granddaddy of them all, the $20 billion fund for victims of the BP Deepwater Horizon oil spill. So how does Feinberg decide what each life is worth? If we are equal, as the UDHR affirms, isn't every life worth the same?

No. At least, not according to the law.

In the case of the September 11 fund, Feinberg writes, "The law required that I give more money to the stockbroker, the bond trader and the banker than to the waiter, the policeman, the fireman and the soldier at the pentagon."[6] For each person who died, Feinberg employed a formula to determine their monetary value. He calculated the income each person would have generated in their lifetime and added more for the pain and suffering they experienced. Ultimately, the value of each person rested entirely on how much they contributed to the economy.

Feinberg has numerous stories of meeting with the loved ones of those who died on September 11. During one meeting, a husband played an audio recording of his wife, who was trapped in one of the doomed towers, saying goodbye. In another, a fireman's widow begged for her check to be fast-tracked because her terminal cancer ensured that her children would be orphaned before the settlement was complete. He has had to sit quietly while grieving families yell at him, accusing him of being unfair. At one public meeting, a grieving husband accused him, saying, "Why not just set a flat number? Why all the calculations? Is my wife worth less than a bond trader? Well, not to me. We were married for thirty-seven years. She's worth a gazillion dollars."[7] As Feinberg listened to these stories, his perspective changed. He writes, "Trained in the law, I had always accepted that no two lives were worth the same in financial terms. But now I found the law in conflict with my growing belief in the equality of all life."[8]

Yet the law prevailed. The families of those at the top of the socioeconomic ladder were awarded an average of $7 million each. Those at the bottom got 96.5 percent less.

We can all sympathize with that grieving husband who was feeling the pain of inequality, and we can also sympathize with Feinberg, who was being accused of inequality while just trying to do his job. The truth is that we all know that placing any monetary value on a human life can never capture its true worth, and that despite what the law says, humans are all equal. Yet the naturalistic worldview doesn't provide any basis for that equality. Instead it sides with the law: of course some people are more valuable than others, because they bring more value to the human race. After all, in the struggle for life, there are always winners and losers.

Christianity teaches that all people are equal creations of God, made in the same image and equally loved. Gregory of Nyssa, a church leader in the fourth century, understood the importance of a Christian worldview in relation to equality. He witnessed the buying and selling of slaves and spoke out against it, writing one of the world's first recorded arguments against slavery. He said, "So when someone turns the property of God into his own property and [assumes] dominion over his own kind, so as to think himself the owner of men and women, what is he doing but overstepping his own nature through pride, regarding himself as something different from his subordinates? . . . For what price, tell me? What did you find in existence worth as much as this human nature? . . . How [much money] did you reckon the equivalent of the likeness of God? How many [dollars] did you get for selling the being shaped by God?"[9]

These questions drive home the point we all know: you can't put a price tag on a human. The very act of assigning a dollar amount to human life is to *de*value human life. Similarly, it's the height of arrogance to buy, sell, or destroy what doesn't belong to you, and humanity doesn't belong to us; it belongs to God. All humans are equally valuable, and yet our pride causes us to puff ourselves up and dehumanize others by making them inferior to ourselves.

GOOD CITIZENS ONLY?

If the UDHR is correct and humans have inherent dignity with value and equality that is not earned, then it also follows that people have inalienable rights. *Inalienable* means that your rights cannot be taken away, changed, or denied. *Rights* refer to the way that humans ought to be treated morally. The idea of human rights being inalienable stems from the idea that they are inherent. If your rights are not given to you by other humans but rather are something that you are simply born with, then it makes sense that other humans can't take them away.

Yet just as a worldview without God can't provide a foundation for inherent dignity and equality, so it likewise falters with the claim of inalienable rights. In a naturalistic worldview like evolutionary biology, nothing is inalienable. That everything slowly changes and evolves is the foundation for understanding the world. If our value as humans is tied to our abilities or capacities, as naturalistic worldviews usually argue, then our moral rights must be tied to those as well.

Mahatma Gandhi was seen by many as a great champion of human rights, and yet even he denied that they were inalienable. For decades, he passionately defended the rights of the Indian people, women, and those with the lowest position in society, the "untouchables." Yet in a letter to the United Nations concerning the UDHR, he wrote the following: "I learnt from my illiterate but wise mother that all rights to be deserved and preserved came from duty well done. Thus the very right to life accrues to us only when we do the duty of citizenship of the world. From this one fundamental statement, perhaps it is easy enough to define the duties of Man and Woman and correlate every right to some corresponding duty to be first performed."[10]

In Gandhi's worldview, human rights don't come from God; they come from being a good person. Therefore, human rights aren't inalienable. They are dependent on a person's performing in a way that society approves of.

If our rights are something that we earn by being a good person, then it casts doubt on huge sections of our society. What about children, including unborn children, who haven't had the time to prove themselves? What about people with mental health challenges who might not understand how to be a good citizen? Have criminals completely lost their human rights? If we receive the right to life only when we fulfill our duties, as Gandhi asserts, then all of the power resides with those in charge, who are given the authority to decide what our duties are and who has fulfilled them. Is that a system that leads to inalienable rights? It sounds more like the system that led to slavery, the eugenics movement, and the gas chambers.

Christianity teaches that humans were created by God and bear his image and that our rights were given to us by him. The Bible also teaches that God's character, his love for us, does not change. His love cannot be lost or taken away from us. In one sense, Gandhi was right in understanding that rights must somehow be earned. However, he was wrong in thinking that we can earn our own rights. Christianity teaches that the moral rights of humans *were* earned, but not by us. God's good character, his holiness, is what gives us our value, equality, and rights, and therefore they can never be taken away.

VISION PROBLEMS

The Universal Declaration of Human Rights got half the story right. It recognizes the truth that all humans have inherent dignity, equality, and inalienable rights, yet it lacks the foundation to explain why it's true. But we can find a solid foundation for believing what our conscience knows to be true in Christianity.

Yet the existence of God doesn't just fix the problem on some philosophical level, as if life is an algebra problem that requires us to plug God in for x in order for the answer to come out right. Our belief in God also affects how we experience human value in our daily lives. As I've reflected on Matlynn's story, I've come to appreciate that the question of human value can be asked from three different perspectives, each challenging in its own right. The first perspective is the value that *we see in others,* the second is the value *we see in ourselves,* and the third is the value *others see in us.* If we want to avoid dehumanization, we need to start by seeing God correctly and then allow that to change how we see ourselves and others.

Let's start with how we value others. We've talked a lot about different ways that our culture, both past and present, has removed God and consequently viewed other people wrongly. But the truth is that Christians are not immune, and they too can get a warped perspective of others. There are many historical examples of Christians leading the charge against dehumanization, but there are also terrible episodes in the history of the church when they have been the ones dehumanizing. Just because people claim to be Christians doesn't mean they live as Christ did.

In the nineteenth century, when King Leopold II was exploiting the Congolese, it was Christians like the minister George Williams who fought against it. He traveled to the Congo to see for himself the "crimes against humanity," a term he coined which helped put an end to those atrocities.[11] That's an example of Christians getting it right. Yet in the same time period, in Canada, a whole lot of Christians were getting it wrong: the Indigenous peoples of Canada were being systematically dehumanized by the Canadian government in cooperation with the church. In 1876 the Indian Act was passed and a cultural genocide began. Nicholas Davin, one of the architects of this racial extermination, explained, "[I]f anything is to be done with the Indian, we must catch him very young. The children must be kept constantly within the circle of civilized conditions."[12] Indigenous children were taken from their families and placed in residential schools. These schools, which were run by Roman Catholic, Anglican, United, Presbyterian, and Methodist churches, were purposely built away from Indigenous communities so that it was difficult for family and friends to visit. How would you feel if the government took your children and kept them away from you? The children were often banned from speaking their ancestral languages, forced to convert to the Christian faith, denied participation in cultural practices, and exposed to various forms of abuse. Duncan Campbell Scott, who worked for the Department of Indian Affairs and was an ardent supporter of residential schools, stated the purpose plainly: "I want to get rid of the Indian problem . . . Our objective is to continue until there is not a single Indian in Canada that has not been absorbed into the body politic."[13]

By disconnecting the children from their parents, communities, culture, and language, the government hoped that Indigenous cultures would disappear over time. The result was gross dehumanization. The residential school system led to widespread abuse and even the deaths of thousands of children. Astonishingly, it wasn't until 1996 that the last school was closed.

When it comes to residential schools, both the Canadian government and the church got it wrong. Their perspective needed to be corrected. Yet seeing the mistakes of others in the past is easy compared with seeing our own mistakes in the present, and so I must confess that I too have found it easy to harbor racism in my heart. Maybe you can relate. How often have you heard one negative story and, in your head, dismissed an entire culture as lazy, dishonest, greedy, or stupid? When we see a person who is struggling with poverty, substance abuse, or criminal behavior, it is tempting to use that example to define an entire group of people. Most of the time we don't question our own prejudices.

It wasn't until I heard a speaker at a conference in Ottawa that my eyes opened to my prejudices. Kenny Blacksmith, an Indigenous leader and a Christian, has worked tirelessly for the reconciliation of the Canadian government, the church, and Indigenous peoples. He spoke about prejudice and ended his talk by offering a hug for those of us who would like to start over. I gladly accepted that hug and my distorted view took the first step toward change. I needed to let my view of God inform how I value others—as people made in his image, with inherent value and dignity.

BIG, BALD, AND BEAUTIFUL

We also need to let our view of God inform how we value ourselves. In some ways, that's even harder. Being secure in our own value is particularly challenging given the comparison culture in which we live today. In our search for self-worth, it's so easy to fall into a trap of comparing ourselves with others. Education, GPA, car, house, age, weight, looks, personality, gender, relationships, marriage, children, career, vacations, wealth, awards. Any of those hit close to home?

I call it a trap because comparing yourself with others is a game you can't win, and if you think you're winning, you're just cheating. There will always be someone smarter, wealthier, and more attractive than you. Working hard isn't bad, and being beautiful is not a sin, but trying to find your value in those things will always lead you to devalue yourself. We pay lip service to the UDHR, claiming that we are all equal, but when we participate in our comparison culture, it's the opposite of equality that we are seeking. Most of the time, we don't worry that we are winning the comparison game; we worry that we are losing—and losing badly.

So what are your insecurities? Where have you become caught in the comparison trap and lost sight of your value?

As a father, I've learned that children have insecurity radar. It's like an innate talent they have for saying exactly the wrong thing at the worst possible time. I'll never forget when my oldest boy had just learned how to speak. He was chatty and unpredictable, a trait my wife and I were sure would cause trouble. One day we took him swimming, and a man with a rather large belly came walking into the pool area. My son pointed at him and, laughing, said in a loud voice, "Hey, Dad—look! A fatty guy." Instantly, the pool went silent. I nearly died right there. The man stopped, turned toward us, and began to walk over. I slowly descended into the water, really wishing that I wasn't in the shallow end. With a serious face, the man came up to my son, pointed at him, and said, "I want to see what your body looks like at sixty-five!" Then the man burst out laughing. Phew—dodged a bullet on that one!

My own insecurities were not spared my children's pokes and prods. They often asked me, "Dad, when did you lose your hair?" Maybe this wasn't just curiosity. Maybe they were concerned for the future of their follicles. I would reassure them, saying, "I came out of the womb balding. I never had a chance." Then, naturally, they asked the follow-up question: "*Why* are you bald?" I would take a moment to collect myself, draw in a deep emotional breath, and then answer in a serious tone, "When the good Lord made me, he accidentally made me too beautiful. Taking pity on mankind, God knew he would need to take my hair from me. I've come to terms with the Lord's decision." Straight faced, I fought back my laughter as they looked at me doubtfully. My wife, Nancy, confirmed their suspicions by laughing out loud. I had to remind her that the joke was on her, since she was the one who married me!

Obviously, I've learned to laugh at being bald. But when I was twenty-one and each morning my pillow was strewn with the casualties of that night's follicle wars, it was no laughing matter. I loved my hair and tried just about every herbal remedy to save my precious locks before male-pattern baldness stole my loved ones. Nothing worked, and in the end my hairline had receded so far back it looked like the beach at low tide, never to return. I finally exchanged a comb for a razor.

The truth is, we've all got things we are insecure about. What's yours? Don't like your weight? Wish you were taller? Wish you were smarter? Had more money? You'll know you've identified it when you don't want to talk about it.

It's easy for me to write about my hair envy, but other issues have been much more difficult to process, including my dyslexia. Honestly, God still has to teach me every day to find my value in him.

MEAN PEOPLE

Remembering where my value comes from has been difficult in this comparison culture we live in, so I can only imagine how hard it must be for Matlynn, and for millions of others with more challenging disabilities, to live in a society that is constantly jockeying for position. I was brokenhearted over losing my hair, but what I felt then doesn't even scratch the surface. There are many people who truly feel like second-class human beings. This is because human value is not only something we place on others or on ourselves, it's also something that other people place on us.

This reality was made brutally clear to me one day when Matlynn and I went to the park near her house in Portland, Oregon. My nephew, Tate, whom Russ and Lisa adopted from Uganda, came along. As soon as we arrived at the river, a drunk man came out of the parking lot and started yelling racial slurs at Matlynn and Tate because of the color of their skin. I remember thinking to myself, "You've gotta be kidding me! These two have gone through so much and you don't like the color of their skin?" I'll never forget the look on Matlynn's face as she looked at me and asked, "Uncle Andy, is that man speaking to me?" I was speechless. The man continued to come toward us aggressively, spewing his hatred. "Why is he saying those things to me?" she asked. It was a great question, made even more poignant by the fact that this man had dark skin too. I guess in our brokenness, no difference in shade is too minor to notice.

A lady in the park had sized up the situation and quickly called the cops. At the end of the confrontation, one of the police officers graciously asked if I would like him to talk with Matlynn and Tate. I politely declined, saying that they didn't fully understand what had happened and I wanted to keep it that way. The police officer replied, "You can't shelter them forever from this kind of stuff." He was right, and I was incredibly naive. Both Matlynn and Tate knew exactly what had happened. This wasn't the first time, and sadly it won't be the last. They had already learned how painful and dehumanizing it can be when others belittle you or reject your value.

Jesus also knew what it felt like to be dehumanized and rejected by others. Throughout his ministry, Jesus was misunderstood, mocked, ridiculed, and falsely accused. In one instance, in Matthew 12, after Jesus healed a man possessed by demons, the Pharisees accused Jesus of working for the prince of demons himself. In other instances, he was accused of sorcery, gluttony, treason, drunkenness, and lying. The insults he received didn't cause him to question his self-worth or build walls of defensive anger, like insults so often cause us to do. Instead, Jesus realized that their accusations revealed just how blind these people were. Their understanding of both God and humans was so warped that they couldn't grasp the truth of who Jesus was. Jesus, however, never lost sight of the truth, and that truth filled him with compassion and love for others.

HUMAN MASTERPIECE

How we view others can't be relied on to determine human value: we all screw up and dehumanize others. How we view ourselves can't be relied on: we all get caught up in the comparison game and wrestle with self-loathing. How others view us especially can't be relied on to determine our value: hurtful memories of how we have been treated can burrow deep and cause pain and shame our whole lives.

So what can be relied on to determine our value?

I have always loved those stories you hear about a person rummaging through an attic or a garage sale and stumbling across a treasure. In 1992, Teri Horton paid five dollars for a painting at a thrift shop. Later, she was asking $50 million for it. Why was there such a huge change in value? Well, it turns out that painting she stumbled on was potentially a previously unknown painting by abstract master Jackson Pollock. Many, myself included, scratch their heads wondering how Pollock's random splashes and dribbles of color can possibly be considered good art. If I had seen that painting at the thrift store, I would have walked right by. Obviously, I'm not an art critic. Art appraisers don't rely on their taste but instead use three rules to determine a painting's value: who created it, what they created, and how much someone is willing to pay for it.

When thinking about human value, it's helpful to use the same questions: Who made it? What did they make? And how much would someone pay for it?

We are worth much more than a painting by a famous artist because we were made by the greatest artist of all—God. He is the source of creativity and beauty in the universe into which every other artist dips their brush. The book of Psalms tells us that the all-knowing, all-powerful, and all-loving one who holds the universe together also knits us together in our mothers' wombs. Of all the things that God made, nothing compares to humanity, because we alone bear his image. It is like his stamp of authenticity, verifying our incomparable worth. Because he created us, we have inherent dignity, equality, and inalienable rights.

An art collector may be willing to pay millions for a painting, even an ugly one, but nothing can compare with what God paid for us. Jesus explained in John 15:12–13 that the most that you can pay for a thing is your life. He said, "Love each other as

I have loved you. Greater love has no one than this: to lay down one's life for one's friends."

That's exactly what Jesus did: he paid for us with his life. Remember the Israelites wandering in the wilderness after God had rescued them from their slavery in Egypt? Well, humankind's slavery to sin was infinitely more hopeless than their situation. We were born into a debt we could never repay. Yet God looked at his masterpiece, the thing of most value among all the things he had created, and when he saw us in bondage, he didn't turn away. Instead, he sent his son, who willingly came to purchase us back. When Jesus Christ died on the cross, he died in our place. His sacrifice was the greatest conceivable demonstration of human value. We are worth much more than some splashes of paint on canvas, because he was willing to pay the ultimate price.

PART 3

WHAT LEADS TO HUMAN FLOURISHING?

5

LONELY PLANET

When I travel, one of my favorite things to do is ride in a taxi and culture-watch through the windows. I find it fascinating, as I weave through the streets of a new city, to peer into people's lives even for just a brief second. Taking in the sights and sounds, I'm reminded that each person I see represents a story within the larger narrative of their culture. Of all the interesting taxi rides I've taken, none was quite as mesmerizing as in Seoul, South Korea. I couldn't help but stare out the window as people busily navigated this technology-rich city.

I had been eagerly looking forward to visiting South Korea. However, in the few weeks previous, my excitement was tempered with some trepidation. North Korea had made world headlines by launching some missiles into the ocean and threatening to send a few to South Korea and North America. Tensions were high, especially considering that North Korea had proven it had an assortment of missiles, nuclear capability, and one of the largest militaries in the world. In fact, my flight to Seoul had taken longer than necessary, detouring through China in order to give North Korea's "supreme commander" Kim Jong-un and his missiles a wide berth.

As the taxi weaved in and out of traffic, I wondered what it must be like for the people in South Korea to live with the constant threat of war, knowing that a bomb could drop with little or no warning.

A TALE OF TWO COUNTRIES

When it comes to the question of human flourishing, the Korean peninsula has come to represent two opposing extremes. North Korea symbolizes the opposite of flourishing. It's a nation held in the grip of totalitarian oppression and a cult of personality that controls every aspect of life. The communist government tightly controls and manipulates its people by restricting their access to information and feeding them a steady dose of propaganda. North Koreans are not allowed to leave their country, or sometimes even their city, and they have no access to the internet. International phone calls, blue jeans, and Christianity are prohibited. The government controls every newspaper and radio station. North Koreans' access to information is so restricted that the government could, and did, claim that Kim Jong-il, the previous leader, invented the hamburger and was the world's leading fashion icon. The government chooses every person's job and also decides what people wear and even what their haircuts can look like. Any offense could have you sent to a labor camp. Not only have the people learned to fear their government but they have also learned to fear each other. The North Korean government monitors their citizens' every move and plants spies in their communities, leaving people with no one to trust. It's a nation held in fear.

It's difficult to imagine being born into that kind of captivity—a land void of freedom, trust, and hope. Combine that with the sanctions and embargoes imposed on the North Korean government and you've got one of the poorest and most technologically deprived nations on the planet. Satellite images taken of the Korean peninsula at night provide a striking visual demonstration of that poverty. China in the north and South Korea in the south are lit up like Christmas trees. In the middle lies North Korea, almost completely black. It's a nation of darkness, both literally and figuratively. Besides a few brave tourists, people are not lining up to go to North Korea. Instead, it's a place that people risk their lives to escape.

But escape to what?

South Korea is the complete opposite of North Korea. It is a democratic nation in which the people are free to travel, communicate, and learn. Incredible public transportation connects South Koreans to each other, and the world's fastest high-speed internet connects South Koreans to the rest of the world. South Korea is famous for its abundance of great food, including Korean BBQ, bibimbap, and kimchi. (Well, maybe not the kimchi. Fermented spicy cabbage may be a delicacy to some, but no thank you.) The capital, Seoul, is one of the most technologically advanced cities in the world; it's one of those places that you visit to peek into the future. To prove this, all I had to do was go to the bathroom in my hotel. The toilet looked like the captain's chair on the *Starship Enterprise*. It had buttons to do just about everything, including calling for help. I know this because a friend of mine accidentally triggered the alarm. It set off flashing lights and a siren throughout the hotel room, followed by a call from the front desk to see if we needed help. That conversation was awkward, but interesting.

HUMAN FLAVOR

What fascinates me about South Korea is that although it is the polar opposite of North Korea, being rich in freedom, food, and technology, it has not led to human flourishing either. This became clear to me as I sat in the back of that taxi. As we neared our destination, my thoughts were cut short when the driver began to speak in Korean. My friend Steve Kim was sitting with the driver in the front. As you can guess from Steve's last name, he's from South Korea. When he was fourteen years old, his parents moved to Canada. His Korean first name is Changbum (pronounced *Chung Bum*). Sadly, they changed it to Steve. I prefer his Korean name and love that his mom still calls him Bum for short.

My point is that although Steve speaks Korean fluently, culturally he's Canadian. So as they talked, the driver brought Steve up to speed on the state of South Korean culture. He explained that the people had much more than war with North Korea to worry about. He told us about the South Korean job market and how fiercely competitive it had become. Given how hard all of my Korean friends had worked during their undergraduate and graduate degrees, I wasn't surprised. Reflecting on his time shuttling people around the city for the last thirty years, our driver told Steve, "The Korean people have lost their *inganmi*."

Steve explained that this Korean word translates literally to "human (*in-gan*) flavor (*mi*)."

"What does he mean that Koreans have lost their human flavor?" I asked. "Does he mean humanity?"

"It's more than that," Steve said. "The word *inganmi* has to do with certain positive qualities that make us more than animals, such as compassion, neighborly love, and selflessness."

Our driver further clarified, saying, "We have been taught to see each other only as competition."

The truth of this cultural shift had been confirmed to us earlier in the week when we had lunch with some Korean young adults. They had shared that given the unemployment levels, competition for jobs had become even more intense, so much so that many were giving up on a career and either settling for a paycheck at some meaningless job or embracing unemployment. If you were employed, the demands of work were all consuming. In Korea, people no longer have the time, money, and desire for things like dating, marriage, and kids. Given these factors, this young adult demographic has been labeled as the generation that has given up on the Big Five: having a career, dating, getting married, owning a home, and having kids. When I was growing up in Portland, Oregon, we called that the American dream. It's a dream that many around the world are giving up.

When I was younger, I too experienced a time when I rejected the dream of coming home from my office with a view to a large house with a white picket fence and being greeted by my beautiful wife, 2.5 kids, and perfectly behaved dog. Instead, I wanted the freedom to travel the world. The American dream felt more like a prison sentence with the twin shackles of mortgage and daycare. I think we all have an idea of what will and will not lead to the best possible life for ourselves. For a while, adventure was where I believed the best possible life could be found.

Giving up on the Big Five has become something of a global phenomenon these days. Maybe you are like me when I was young and think, "What's the big deal? Maybe those traditional values are outdated and not worth pursuing in the modern world."

To answer that, let's consider this idea of human flavor. Scientists tell us that 80 percent of the flavor we taste in our food comes from our sense of smell and that flavor is essential not only to our enjoyment of food but also to our satisfaction with life. When people lose their sense of smell, and thus flavor, it affects their feeling of hunger and can lead to detrimental weight loss, impaired immunity, and poor nutrition. One man who lost his sense of smell from an accident in 2005 described his life to a reporter from the BBC: "It's so hard to explain but losing your sense of smell leaves you feeling like a spectator in your own life, as if you're watching from behind a pane of glass. It makes you feel not fully immersed in the world around you and sucks away a lot of the colour of life. It's isolating and lonely."[1]

Studies support his conclusions. Those who have lost their ability to detect flavor show a huge increase in stress, anger, and isolation and report that it negatively affects both their safety and their personal relationships. One study showed that losing the ability to detect flavor leads to longer and more intense periods of depression than blindness.

So what did my cab driver mean when he talked about human flavor? He meant the things that make life worth living, the things that give us pleasure, meaning, and satisfaction. What are those things? What leads to human flourishing?

I HEART SCREEN TIME

The South Koreans I talked with effortlessly rattled off a bunch of things that people saw as giving life flavor—dating, marriage, having kids—and they all spoke candidly about how these things had lost their appeal and, thus, they were rejecting them. Yet what I found interesting is that none of these people really dove into why they were giving up on these things and what they were choosing to replace them with. After all, it's easy to misunderstand all this talk about marriage and babies and forget that these are only symptoms of a bigger issue. People all over the world aren't just giving up dreams of white picket fences, they are giving up on relationships in general. Why?

They are giving up on relationships in general because they have given up on one relationship in particular: a relationship with God.

As the creator of human life, God is the one who knows what will lead to human flourishing. The story of the Bible tells us over and over that God made humans to flourish in relationship, with him and with each other. So when the modern world chose to reject God, it started a trajectory that led to a rejection of relationship with one another as well. To bring in our metaphor of flavor, we can think of God as the one who gives us our sense of smell and taste. If he disappears, it only makes sense that all of the good flavors he gave us, things like the Big Five, would lose their luster as well.

In South Korea, the problem has become critical. The young adults there told me that they are no longer called the generation that has given up on the Big Five. They are now called the generation that has given up on everything.

Well, almost everything.

They haven't given up on technology.

Remember the previous chapter when we talked about how our gods write their names on our faces? Humans were made to worship, and if we refuse to worship God, we will eventually worship something else as a god replacement. In our modern culture, technology has become that god. Technology is seen as the thing that will give our lives meaning, that will define our humanity, and that will lead to our flourishing.

But what's especially interesting about technology as a god replacement is that technology is something under our control. As the makers of technology, we can choose to craft it however we like. So what kind of god are we creating?

Modern technology often reminds me of the story of Narcissus from Greek mythology. The details of the story vary from source to source, but the basic storyline remains the same. A man of great beauty bends over a pool of water and upon seeing his reflection becomes so captivated that he falls in love with himself. Unable to leave the beauty of his reflection, Narcissus eventually loses the will to live. He just stares at his reflection until he dies.

Something profoundly similar to this is taking place in the twenty-first century through our technology. Nothing in history has reflected our image more clearly and captured our attention as profoundly as our technology. Like Narcissus, we are enamored with ourselves, and so we craft technology that shows our own reflection. Rather than God creating humans in his image, we can now make god in our image.

With technology as our god, technology likewise becomes the answer to what will lead to human flourishing. The truth is that our culture hasn't really given up on things like the Big Five. Instead, we attempt to fulfill those human longings while keeping our focus on ourselves, and technology makes that possible. Don't want the hassle of dating, the challenges of marriage, or the career-killer of children? Technology promises to solve all of our relational needs quickly, conveniently, and hassle free. Need a friend? There's social media and chatbots for that. Need intimacy? There's pornography and robot sex for that. Want a child? There's a video game for that, even an app to see what they would look like and virtual reality goggles to interact with them.

Is it working? Is this leading to greater human flourishing? Is our technology making us more human or less?

MODERN FAMILY

One of the first human flavors that our modern society has given up on is the desire for children. It is a perspective that can be seen in nearly every affluent country, and it's having a dramatic effect. Consumer cultures around the world are failing to sustain their nations' populations. Each country needs a birth rate of at least 2.1 to keep its population stable. But most affluent countries are not even close to that and, as a result, require mass immigration to offset their lack of children. In their book *Empty Planet,* authors Bricker and Ibbitson argue that although we've been taught to believe that the earth will be overpopulated in the future, the opposite is taking place.[2]

Singapore is the perfect example of this global trend. As of

2016, Singapore's birth rate was the lowest in the world at 1.2, competing with Germany, Japan, South Korea, and Hungary. Thus far, nothing has worked to encourage Singaporeans to bring forth life. The government of Singapore became so desperate for babies they even teamed up with the company Mentos to make a video and catchy rap song to promote a campaign called National Night. The idea behind the campaign is that everyone will use Singapore's national independence day, August 9, as a time to do their "civic duty" of procreating. Rap lyrics include gems like, "Let's not watch fireworks, let's make 'em instead. Singapore's population, it needs some increasin'. So forget waving flags, August 9 we freakin'."[3] Astonishingly, not even Mentos, a catchy song, and a viral YouTube video could get people pregnant.

So instead, Singapore stepped it up a notch. They now offer large cash incentives for having children. Germany took a more subtle approach through monthly subsidies, paid maternity leave, and a national daycare service. Hungary, getting downright desperate and creative, in 2019 started offering tax exemptions for life and subsidies for larger cars to women who have four or more children. Yet none of these strategies have been successful, and, frankly, if they were, those are not the people you want having kids! Imagine that tender moment playing out when little Jimmy asks, "Hey, Mom, why did you and Dad have us four kids?" and she replies, "For the tax benefits, sweetie."

Clearly, people's motivations for making babies run deeper than national pride or economics.

What surveys continue to show is that people in the developing world are rethinking the physical, emotional, and financial burdens of having children. A 2015 Israeli study by Orna Donath showed that many women regret motherhood, even though they love their children. She writes, "[O]ne of the central themes in contemporary mothers' accounts on motherhood, especially during the first years of infancy: loss. That is, loss of self and the sense of freedom and control, as well as loss of time."[4] Having an adult child is great, but all the work of parenting, wiping bums and runny noses, is no fun. In Germany, a 2016 Yougov survey reached the same conclusion, showing that one in five mothers regrets having children, nearly half reporting that this is because children are a career killer.[5] In all of the material I could find on maternal regret, children were viewed as a burden with very little payoff. Donath writes, "Thus, all of the women in my study concluded that as far as they are concerned, the disadvantages outweigh the benefits. Moreover, several of them said that for them there is nothing benign about the maternal experience but rather they see it as 'adding virtually nothing to life, apart from perpetual difficulty and worry.'"[6]

All of the women in the study insisted that they loved their children, but that in their cost-benefit analysis, love wasn't strong enough to outweigh the negatives.

IT'S A GIRL!

In China, the government chose a route opposite to that of Singapore, Germany, and Hungary by preceding their people in the devaluing of children. Starting in 1970, the government started encouraging Chinese people to marry later in life and to have only two children. When that failed to curb population growth, stricter measures were brought in, and on September 18, 1980, the One Child Policy came into effect. It required anyone desiring to have a child to obtain a birth permit. Birth permits were given only to married couples who had no children. All pregnancies occurring without a permit were forcibly terminated or the parents were heavily fined.

The result for China has been anything but the utopia they were hoping for. Chinese authorities claim to have prevented approximately 400 million births between 1979 and 2011. The One Child Policy, a cultural bias toward sons, and the advancement of prenatal screening technology formed a deadly combination. Sex-selective abortion and infanticide of baby girls skyrocketed in China. During the One Child Policy, the three most dangerous words in China were "It's a girl."

The result of this dehumanization of baby girls has led to a huge imbalance in the number of men versus women in China. It has been estimated that there are 40 million young men in China unable to find a female partner with whom to start a family because those females don't exist. The future for China is that one in five Chinese men will be forced to become a "bare branch," a biological dead end on the genealogical tree. Already this gender imbalance has been linked to an increase in violent crime, crimes against women, substance abuse, gangs, sex trafficking, and suicide.

Beyond creating a gender imbalance, China's policies encouraged the Chinese to adopt a perspective that has left little to no desire for more children. In 2016, the One Child Policy in China was officially amended to a Two Child Policy. However, by that time, the culture's perspective on marriage and children had changed drastically. Rather than jump at the opportunity to have more children, most Chinese couples are adopting the attitude of the rest of the industrialized world and second-guessing whether it is worth it to have any children at all.

When we ignore God and instead focus on ourselves, we inevitably deny the things that he says give life value, including creating life. The Bible repeatedly teaches that children are a blessing and not a burden. Psalm 127:3 says, "Children are a heritage from the LORD, offspring a reward from him." Yet in answering the question of what leads to human flourishing, our culture has given up on children because we've given up on the concept that sacrifice could be good for you, that human flourishing includes taking your focus off of yourself and attending to the needs of others. Instead, we've given up on children and relationships in general. The result hasn't been a thriving of the human race. We have stopped seeing children as humans and started seeing them as burdens, barriers on the path to financial success or individual fulfillment and freedom. In China, this attitude led to the dehumanization of baby girls and the deaths of millions, and around the world the giving up of children is slowly leading to the deaths of entire cultures as their populations disappear with each passing year. Is that what it means for humanity to flourish?

Today's culture says children don't lead to flourishing—technology does. So, as with all human desires, we now take the desire for children and try to satisfy it with technology. That's exactly the desire that a now-defunct video game called Prius tapped into. A primary component of the game was an Anima, a childlike creature that each player was given to raise. One Korean couple became so obsessed with raising their virtual child that they forgot to feed their real child. Their infant daughter, only a few months old, died of starvation and neglect.[7]

As sad as that story is, what's even sadder is that it isn't the only one. Stories about parents nurturing their technology addiction instead of their children have also popped up in the United States, Australia, and England. Even if some of these stories turn out to be rumors or exaggerations, their very existence reveals that we all know the truth: technology can't replace real relationships. It can't replace children. Even the attempt, when seen in the stark pages of your newsfeed, seems horrifying to us.

Equally troubling is the growing trend of having kids, only to outsource the raising of those children to technology. Screen time has become a parental substitute. Getting down on the floor and playing with your toddler takes more effort than letting them watch another adult unbox toys on YouTube.

Having a conversation with your child is more challenging than handing them your phone or streaming another episode. We aren't surprised when study after study shows the detrimental effects of too much technology on children, and yet this is still something that all parents struggle with. Even though we know that children need real relationships, it is still so tempting to substitute those with technology.

ROBOT SPOUSE

Even when faced with the horrifying results, we continue to turn a blind eye to the truth of human flourishing and choose instead to give up on human relationships, replacing them with more and more technology. It's not just children we are giving up on. It's also marriage, dating, and friendships. All types of basic human interaction have now gone digital.

The extent to which we have outsourced our humanity became clear to me one day when I saw a commercial from a Japanese company called Gatebox.[8] In the commercial, a single Japanese man wakes up in his small apartment to a cheerful voice greeting him: "It's morning! Wake uuuup!" The voice comes from a cute hologram of an anime-like character that resides in a glass case beside his bed. She has blue hair and wears a short white dress with long stockings. As the man gets ready for the day, she continually interacts with him, reminding him to take an umbrella because it will rain today and playfully chiding him to hurry up or he will be late. As he leaves, she sweetly says goodbye. On his commute and during his long day at the office, he has no human conversation. But his little anime girlfriend texts back and forth with him. She tells him that she misses him and hopes that he can come home early. Sadly, he can't; it's going to be another long day at the office. As he leaves work that night, it's raining and he pulls out his umbrella, grateful for all the tiny details she has taken care of. When he arrives at his apartment, she has the lights on and the temperature adjusted just the way he likes it. In the evening, they share a hot beverage and watch some TV together, him drinking out of a real mug and her out of a little hologram one. As he crawls into bed, he reflects on the day, saying, "You know, somebody's home for me. Feels great."

It's a strange commercial. The first time I saw it, I laughed. But my laughter died when I realized that it wasn't a joke. This product is for sale in Japan. In December 2018, a man in Japan even hosted a marriage ceremony for him and his virtual wife. Now, there is no doubt that real human husbands and wives are more complicated than holograms. Relationships with actual human beings require humility, patience, compassion, and forgiveness. But isn't it worth it? Aren't those relationships part of what make us human?

Maybe the thought of a hologram spouse isn't attractive to you. Maybe there is another relational itch that needs to be scratched. Don't worry, I'm sure there's an app for that. After all, with internet porn, immersive online video games, and social media networks, it seems so easy to find all of the excitement, connection, and sexual gratification we need instantly, privately, and effortlessly. Compared with the ease of the internet, real relationships are full of risk, effort, and financial strain.

The existence of one type of technology perhaps hasn't even crossed your mind, yet a bill about it was passed in the US House of Representatives in June 2017. The bill is called the CREEPER Act. CREEPER stands for Curbing Realistic Exploitative Electronic Pedophilic Robots.[9] The goal of the bill is to restrict the sale of sex robots that have been designed to look like children. What is most interesting about the bill is that it causes us to think seriously about where we draw the lines of what is acceptable and what is not. If we are okay with replacing human spouses with technology, like Gatebox is attempting to do, then is it okay to replace human sexual relationships with technology? If so, can we make them look however we want? Is it okay to make a sex robot that looks like a child? What about making it look like a specific child, like your neighbor's kid? It's repulsive to think about, but it is more than possible.

OUTSOURCING HUMANITY

In its stubborn refusal to acknowledge God, our culture ends up chasing after the wind, trying to fill any need we have with gods of our making. The result hasn't been for our flourishing, but for our harm. When I think of that Gatebox commercial, or any other of the many TV shows and movies that depict our relationship to technology, I am reminded that even in the midst of the information age, loneliness is at an all-time high. It has become an epidemic around the world. It has become so bad that in 2019, the prime minister of the UK created a new position: the Minister of Loneliness.[10] The decision was prompted by research that has shown the health benefits of relationships and the health dangers of loneliness. One study in 2017 showed that loneliness is a health crisis worse than the risk from alcohol consumption, obesity, and air pollution.[11] It reported that the effects of loneliness are equivalent to smoking fifteen cigarettes a day.

In Japan, loneliness, particularly among the elderly, has become such a problem that an entirely new word has been coined: *kodokushi* means "lonely death" and refers to the growing phenomenon of people who are so cut off from human relationships and interactions that when they die alone in their apartments, no one knows about it.[12] Bodies can remain undiscovered for months and sometimes years. The first case to get media coverage was a sixty-seven-year-old man who had been lying dead on his floor for three years before anyone noticed. His rent and other bills had been withdrawing automatically from his bank account, and it was only when the account ran dry that someone thought to check on him. It is estimated that tens of thousands of *kodokushi* deaths happen every year in Japan.

What do we do when faced with stories like this? We use technology, of course. If we have a human need, something that is standing in the way of our flourishing, technology can meet it! This is the impulse driving the development of sociable robots. Sociologist Sherry Turkle describes an interaction with one such robot in her book *Reclaiming Conversation*. Paro is a "therapeutic robot" designed primarily to provide calm companionship for people in nursing homes. Shaped like a baby seal, Paro's soft fur and large black eyes give it a cuddly appearance. It moves, blinks, and responds to touch and the human voice. In the course of her research, Turkle often brought these robots into nursing homes. She was amazed at the benefits to the elderly, who just needed someone to talk to and touch. The researchers would stand around, in awe of how they were helping these people with their technology. Then, one day, she saw something that changed her mind. An elderly woman opened up to the little seal about a child she had lost. The seal appeared empathetic and engaged and the lady responded, pouring out her heart to the fuzzy little robot. Everyone was amazed. But, Turkle writes, "I didn't find it amazing. I felt we had abandoned this woman . . . There were so many people there to help, but we all stood back, a room of spectators now, only there to hope that an elder would bond with a machine. It seemed that we all had a stake in outsourcing the thing we do best—understanding each other, taking care of each other."[13]

At the conclusion of her book, Turkle gets to the heart of the matter: "Now we have to ask if we become more human when we give our most human jobs away."[14]

It's an interesting question. What is it that makes us human and what truly leads to our flourishing? When we outsource relationship to technology, what we are really doing is outsourcing our humanity. There's a reason why we are tempted to create machines and software that are human-like. In her earlier book *Alone Together,* Turkle came to the same conclusion after years of research. She said, "Technology is seductive when what it offers meets our human vulnerabilities. And as it turns out, we are very vulnerable indeed. We are lonely but fearful of intimacy."[15] These vulnerabilities are the reason why we give our technology human names and human voices and infuse them with human-like personalities. The goal behind virtual assistants like Apple's Siri or Amazon's Alexa is for us to pretend that they are human, and the truth is, we want to be convinced.

As we create machines that are more and more human-like, it's easy to forget that it also works the other way, making us more and more machine-like. By removing ourselves from relationships with other people, we are dehumanizing ourselves. Turkle expresses her concern with the direction artificial intelligence is going, saying, "I believe that sociable technology will always disappoint because it promises what it cannot deliver. It promises friendship but can only deliver performances. Do we really want to be in the business of manufacturing friends that will never be friends?"[16]

Everything from entertainment, community, and even sexual intimacy can be manufactured to meet our needs. But does it? Research continues to show that our technology doesn't satisfy. It leaves us increasingly insecure, anxious, isolated, and lonely. How do you feel after you've scrolled your Instagram feed for an hour? Uplifted? Probably not.

Now understand, I don't think technology is really the problem here. I think *we* are. Technology itself isn't wrong. It's what we are doing with our technology. I like watching movies, driving my car, and taking medicine when I get sick. I like email and FaceTime and the Uber app. Yet I also feel the pull to spend more and more of my time with my devices instead of with my family and friends. I too am drawn to the convenience of an online life, stripped of the mess and curated to my preferences. This isn't a new problem. It's just revealing what has always been lurking in the human heart. The truth is that instead of loving God with all our heart, soul, mind, and strength, as Deuteronomy 6 instructs us to do, we love ourselves. Most of the time, we don't create technology that helps us to worship God and better reflect his image. Instead, we make technology that mirrors our own image, and we are captivated by it. Like Narcissus, we will stare at that screen until we die. We will never be fully human or treat others as fully human in a way that leads to our flourishing and theirs until we take our focus off of ourselves and put it onto God.

HUMAN FLAVOR

Remember that taxi ride I took in South Korea? Well, I had plenty of time to think that day because our taxi driver got lost. We drove around and around the streets of Seoul, seemingly at random, until our driver finally stopped to call someone for help. I was starting to give up hope that we would ever get there when we finally pulled over on the side of a busy commercial road. Small stores and restaurants crowded the street, with office buildings and apartments rising above them. There was nothing in sight that looked remotely like a church to me. I turned back to the driver in despair that we were still lost when to my surprise, he pointed up. The modern office building behind us was it: Jusarang Community Church. A man came out to greet us and confirmed that we were in the right place. It did not look like a typical church, but maybe that was fitting, because the ministry of Jusarang isn't typical either. We were there to meet and interview Pastor Jong-rak Lee, a man made famous from a documentary about his life and work called *The Drop Box*.[1]

Steve and I were led up a couple of flights of stairs to where Pastor Lee was waiting in his office. Pastor Lee greeted Steve and me warmly and asked us to take a seat on a small green couch facing a wall lined with bookshelves. Even by Asian standards, the office was tiny. There was barely enough room for us all, which made for an intimate setting to begin our conversation. It also illustrated to me what Pastor Lee really cares about. Some pastors become famous for the beauty and size of their churches or the important books they've written, but not Pastor Lee. He is not a megachurch pastor or a bestselling author. Pastor Lee is famous for loving and caring for abandoned children.

As we talked, Pastor Lee told me the story that began this work. His second child, Eunman Lee, is severely disabled and spent the first fourteen years of his life in the hospital before Pastor Lee and his wife were able to bring him home. Around that time, an elderly lady approached Pastor Lee and his wife with her granddaughter, who was suffering from a condition similar to their son's. In desperation, she asked the Lees if they would consider taking in the girl as well. Initially, Pastor Lee did not even entertain this request. They were pouring so much time and energy into caring for their own son. How could they take in another? But then the grandmother added, "If you take care of this child for me, I will believe in Jesus." Pastor Lee told me, "I couldn't turn this down."

Pastor Lee led us out of his office and showed us around the church as we continued to talk. Walking through the church building, I found myself thinking about his story. Truthfully, I wasn't sure what to think. The cynic in me doubted that the grandmother would actually follow Jesus, and yet Pastor Lee was willing to take that chance. The church now has a medical facility that cares for disabled children. There he introduced me to his son and his adopted daughter. It was one thing to hear his story, but to actually see that he is still taking care of her was powerful. Although she is now an adult, her physical disabilities have left her legs unresponsive. I watched as he got down on the floor with her, and it was obvious that he loved her. Seeing how Pastor Lee loved and cared for the disabled children at his church, I was amazed at his devotion to the gospel and love for people. It reminded me of a conversation I once had with the father of a disabled child. He told me something that really challenged me. He explained how often people ignore the disabled, to the extent that people didn't even make eye contact with his daughter, and how dehumanizing that felt. It's interesting how important those small things are. Now I'm sure to make eye contact and say hi to people, especially those whom our culture tends to ignore. As Pastor Lee loved these kids, he clearly saw and treated them with the dignity they deserve as beings created by God and made in his image.

As he continued to show us around the church, Pastor Lee explained that word eventually got out about what he had done for the grandmother. People began to leave their children at the doors of the church. One day he received a phone call from a father who had left his newborn son outside. Pastor Lee raced out to find a box being circled by alley cats. As he shooed the animals away, he looked inside the box and found a baby turning blue from the cold. He took the child home and nursed him back to health. After this incident, he began to fear that a child could die at his doorstep.

Pastor Lee drove us a short distance to his house. He led us around the side to show us the baby box that he had installed into the wall of his home. The door of the box is painted with classic Asian grammar, "Jesus Love You," and the verse reference "Psalm 27:10." Later, I looked up the verse in my Bible. It says, "Though my father and mother forsake me, the LORD will receive me." The door opens to a heated compartment with bedding and a motion sensor. The box is connected to the inside of the house and alerts people when a child has been placed inside.

After seeing the baby box and hearing his story, we went inside where Pastor Lee introduced me to a beautiful baby boy, about two weeks old, who had been abandoned that morning. As I stared at his beautiful little features, the gravity of it all hit me.

What could drive a parent to abandon their baby? I was broken for that child and his parents. I was also surprised. Considering how this had all begun, I anticipated that the children being abandoned had disabilities, but this child did not. Pastor Lee informed me that the vast majority of the children abandoned do not have a disability and that despite South Korea's very low birth rate, it has a staggeringly high number of babies who are abandoned. Genuinely confused, I asked, "Why do so many parents in South Korea give up their babies?" He explained that there was no simple answer, but that mostly it came down to shame.

Shame affects all people, and there is no greater demonstration of its power than its ability to lead a parent to abandon their child. In 2012, South Korea passed a new law that banned anonymity for parents wishing to give up their children for adoption. Now, both the mother and the father have to register their names with the government. In a shame-based culture like South Korea, this requirement for documentation not only was seen as bringing shame on the family but also provided a way for the child to track the parents down someday. By abandoning their babies, desperate mothers and fathers hope to avoid this shame. When Pastor Lee's drop box opened in 2010, three or four babies were dropped off each month. After the law changed, that figure multiplied eight times. When I was there in 2018, they were averaging four or five babies per week and as many as two babies a day.

As Pastor Lee showed me around, it was clear that his family no longer lived in the house. He explained that as the number of babies increased, the space needed for supplies and volunteers grew until it took over every room in the house. After everything his family had given up for these children, it was humbling to think that it even required their home. As the ministry grew, Pastor Lee began to proactively help single moms and struggling families keep their children. They help by providing supplies, counseling, and even a place to stay. After they moved out of their house, the Lees renovated the space to provide apartments for single mothers and families to help them get back on their feet. They are doing everything they can to keep these babies with their families, and it's working. They have helped many families stay together and are hopeful that one day the culture of South Korea will change so that the baby box will no longer be needed.

SALT OF THE EARTH

Leaving Pastor Lee's house, I found myself reflecting once again on what the taxi driver had said about people in South Korea losing their human flavor. He felt that his culture was losing distinctly human qualities like compassion, neighborly love, and selflessness that are essential for the flourishing of humankind. Instead, he saw people giving up on relationships with others, becoming obsessed with themselves, and losing the flavor and meaning of life along the way. Yet here I had just met a family and a church in that same culture that were full of human flavor. Where did this difference come from?

I was reminded of a famous sermon that Jesus once preached called the Sermon on the Mount, where he touched on this idea of flavor. Chapter 5 of Matthew's gospel records Jesus sitting on a hillside and telling his students or disciples, "You are the salt of the earth."[2] In ancient times, salt was used for many different things. It was an important food preservative in a time before refrigeration. It was occasionally used as a fertilizer or a disinfectant. But the primary use for salt back then was the same as the primary use for salt now: as a flavor enhancer.

The interesting thing about salt as a food additive is that when used in the proper amount, it does not actually make the food taste salty. Instead, it makes the food taste more like itself.

That's why we call it a flavor enhancer. Salt isn't adding a new flavor so much as it is enhancing the flavor that was meant to be there all along. It's almost as if the human tongue has lost some of its ability to detect the true nature of food, and salt helps it regain that ability. So tossing some salt into a tomato sauce makes it taste more tomatoey. Adding salt to a nice juicy steak makes it taste more like a steak. I've even been amazed at friends who swear by sprinkling salt on a slice of watermelon, although I haven't been bold enough to try it myself! They claim it makes the watermelon taste sweeter and purer, more like how a watermelon is meant to taste.

So when Jesus told his followers that they were the salt of the earth, what he was saying is actually similar to what that taxi driver was talking about. Jesus meant that on our own, without God, humans have lost their flavor; human life no longer tastes the way that he created it to. That's why a life without God always leads to dehumanization—a tasteless world. Yet following Jesus acts like salt, restoring life's flavor and our humanness. Human flourishing is like chicken soup. I once made chicken soup from a can, but the taste was so bad I nearly spit it out. Normally, I loved this soup, so I went hunting through the recycling for the can and reread the label. Turns out I had accidentally bought the low-sodium version. Pulling my salt shaker off the shelf, I took a moment to mourn for all of those people in the world who need to lower their sodium intake, and then I salted my soup back to life. Just as chicken soup flourishes when we add salt, so also Jesus restores the human flavor that leads to our flourishing and the flourishing of others.

FUNHOUSE MIRRORS

The Bible tells us that we flourish when we rightly reflect the image of God in which we were created, and that if we want to know what God looks like, we are to look to his son, Jesus. I once heard a story about famous Scottish theologian T. F. Torrance, who served as a chaplain in World War II. Torrance was on the front lines in Italy attending to the wounded when he came across a young man dying of his wounds. Knowing that he was dying and would soon meet God, the young man became afraid. Looking to Torrance, he asked, "What's God like?" The theologian responded, "Look at the face of Jesus. That's exactly what God is like."[3]

This is what the apostle Paul taught in Colossians, saying, "The Son is the image of the invisible God."[4] The writer of the book of Hebrews states, "The Son is the radiance of God's glory and the exact representation of his being."[5] John, a disciple who spent years following Jesus and listening to his teaching, says in the beginning of his gospel, "No one has ever seen God, but the one and only Son, who is himself God and is in closest relationship with the Father, has made him known."[6] These passages teach us that Jesus is both perfectly God and perfectly human. He clearly reflected God's image and is our model for what it means to be human. When we consider what a flourishing life looks like, we are meant to look to the life of Jesus.

This is an important point that we often get wrong. Instead of looking to Jesus, we often look to successful and famous people as our example to follow, only to become confused and disillusioned when their lives fall apart. In today's social-media-saturated world, we're tempted to follow some perfect person or family online and secretly hold them up as the pinnacle of human flourishing: they are living the best possible life filled with adventurous snorkeling trips, magazine-worthy kitchens, model-beautiful children, and the expert-level photography skills needed to capture it all for Instagram. When reality hits and it turns out that all those photos were staged, that the influencer is hiding their depression, that the perfect couple is actually separated, and that the adventurous trips were paid for with crippling debt, we're left feeling deceived and bitter. If those perfect lives aren't actually perfect, then what's the point of it all?

Christians like me can sometimes have our own particular form of this illusion. We spiritualize it, but it's the same problem. Instead of celebrities, we idolize pastors, Christian leaders, and even Bible characters as models for a flourishing life, only to be disappointed just the same. We'll look to people like Abraham, the father of the Jewish nation, as our example of faithfulness, and then read a few chapters further and learn that he was a coward who willingly offered up his wife as a concubine to a foreign king, not once but twice.[7] Abraham was scared for his own neck, and instead of trusting God, he threw his wife to the wolves. Should that be our standard of faithfulness? Yet while Abraham isn't faithful, God is. What makes Abraham great isn't that he was perfect but that he learned to trust that God is good and faithful.

Another favorite for Christians is King David, "a man after God's own heart."[8] He is often lifted up as the poster child for human flourishing. The problem is, David's a train wreck! Sure, David shows immense faith in God, but he still falls prey to the lusts of his heart. He sleeps with another man's wife, gets her pregnant, and then arranges for her husband, a good guy, to be killed in order to cover his tracks. That's not someone you want to model your life after! However, at the same time, David *is* someone we should look up to, because in his mess he realizes how desperately he needs God's mercy and grace.

People often think that the God of the Old Testament is different from the God of the New Testament, but the truth is that it's the same God. The difference is that in the Old Testament, God is working in and through broken people and horrible circumstances, which can make it difficult to clearly see what God is like. God hadn't fully shown himself to his people yet. People like Abraham and David were trying to reflect his image, but usually they were more like those funhouse mirrors at carnivals and haunted houses. Have you ever stood in front of one of those? It's amazing how a few little dents or curves can distort the whole image, giving you a gigantic nose or super-stretched-out arms and legs. Humans like Abraham and David usually reflected God's character like that, getting it right in some places and then horribly wrong in others. That's one of the reasons God sent his son, Jesus, so that we don't have to rely on those poor reflections to see what God is like. If we want to know what God looks like in his character, we can look at Jesus, and if we want to reflect God's image more fully, we can become more like Jesus.

GARDENING TIPS

So if flourishing comes when we reflect God's image, and if God's image is clearly seen in the person of Jesus, then the next question that follows is what does Jesus look like? Jesus' character reveals that God is relational and is committed to relationship. Jesus loved the Father and he sacrificed everything to love other people. Even atheists and people of other religions who deny the deity of Jesus still usually acknowledge that his life on earth was the embodiment of compassion. Jesus cared for all people, even the outcasts, the poor, the sinners, and those abandoned by society.

The Bible teaches that God's nature is that of relationship. His very being embodies relationship because he is the Father, the Son, and the Holy Spirit, three in one. Christians call this the Trinity. It's a difficult concept to grasp, because humans have one nature and are one person. Yet the Bible teaches us that God is different from us. Although he is one, he is also three—three persons sharing one nature. Although this is strange for us to wrap our minds around, the implications of the Trinity are vitally important because it means that God is love.

When the apostle John says in his first letter that "God is love," he is saying not that love is God but rather that God's nature is intrinsically loving.[9] Twelfth-century Scottish theologian Richard of St. Victor argued that in order for God to be loving, he must be triune. He reasoned that if God were only one person, God could not be intrinsically loving because before he created people there would have been, for all eternity, nobody to love. He also realized that if God were only two persons, the fullness of generous love would be lacking. We've all seen two people who are so infatuated with each other that they ignore everyone else, and we intuitively realize how unhealthy that is. True love must be shared and reciprocated. This is what Richard of St. Victor meant when he said, "That love must be mutual is required by the fact that supreme happiness cannot exist without the mutuality of love."[10] Yet if God is three persons, as the Bible describes, God would be perfectly loving in a healthy and generous way that is delighted to share that love.

The implication of the Trinity is that people have been created in a relational image and thus when God made mankind, he made us with relational needs. The book of Genesis tells us the story of how God made the first man, Adam, and put him in a beautiful garden filled with all kinds of amazing plants and animals. Yet despite the perfection of this garden, there was still a problem. Genesis 2:18 says, "The LORD God said, 'It is not good for the man to be alone.'" Adam was in the most amazing place on earth, but he was lonely. So in response to this, God does a strange thing. He takes all the animals that he has made and parades them before Adam so that Adam can name them. Once this is done, Genesis tells us, "But for Adam no suitable helper was found."[11] So God made a woman as the perfect mate for Adam. What? Was making another human God's last resort? Did God really think that an elephant or a turtle would be a good companion instead? Of course not! God was running through the options not for his own benefit but for Adam's. He was showing Adam that animals are wonderful but that he was made for relationship with other persons, that nothing on this earth can satisfy us the way that relationship with God *and* relationship with other humans can.

When I think about the garden of Eden, I am reminded of my garden. It's a curious thing, but the older I get, the more attracted I am to hanging baskets. Each spring, I take a trip to a greenhouse, looking to purchase plants for my yard. I'm a novice when it comes to gardening, so I appreciate the little tag each plant comes with that explains what will lead to its flourishing. Some need full sun and some need shade. Each plant has specific requirements in terms of soil, water, and even neighboring plants. Unless I take into account what will lead to each plant's flourishing, it will eventually wither and die. I know because I have killed many plants this way, thinking I can force it to thrive in a place it's just not suited for.

Humans are the same way. Imagine that each baby is born with a little gardening tag tied around its wrist. What would it say? Each plant has different environmental preferences, but ultimately they all need light, water, and soil to survive. Likewise, each human is born with different tastes, opinions, and interests. But we all need relationships to flourish. Relationships with God and people are like the sun and water, without which we will wither and die.

WHY CHURCH?

In light of how God created us, it should not surprise us, then, that Christianity teaches that people were created for the purpose of creating communities, the kind of communities that are built from generous love that rejoices to be shared with others. This is why I love church so much and also why I get so frustrated with dysfunctional churches or Christians who say they don't need church. A church that does not love and serve each other is not a church, and a person who is not committed to community with God *and* his people is not a Christian.

Once I was speaking at a conference and, after my talk, a lady came up to me to ask some questions. After listening to her for a while, I felt prompted to ask, "Do you like your church?" That question was like a needle to a water balloon. She burst into tears. Given her response, I gently followed it by asking, "Do your kids like to go to church?" With tears running down her cheeks, she looked up at me, shook her head no, and said, "Every week they ask not to go." My heart broke for her. As we talked, it was clear that her church was not a lifegiving community of love but a dead community of obligations.

I have met far too many people who continue to attend broken churches like that one. I've also met a lot of broken people who never commit to a healthy church. A healthy church isn't a church without conflict; it's a church that is so committed to relationship with God and people that it will do the hard work of reconciling relationships when conflict comes. When you hurt someone, make it right. When there's conflict, don't avoid it.

One day a young adult raced up to speak with me after our church service. She had moved here for university, and now that the school year was over, she was returning home to a different city. She wanted to thank me before she left. She said, "God answered my prayers through this church." She had come to our church with no friends and found a community of people who loved God and loved each other, and it changed her life. She experienced human flourishing for the first time in her life, and she was scared to leave. As we prayed together, I reminded her that she is the salt Jesus spoke of. She will return home with the flavor of healthy community to be a light in her city. This is why I love hosting a community group in my house. I have seen so many lives flourish in and through community. People often forget that the good news of the gospel is that we have been saved not only into a personal relationship with God but also into a corporate relationship. When I attend church, I go with the knowledge that I need them and they need me. Together we are the family of God, and, yes, there are some people who require extra grace, but that's what families are like, and when we get it right, it's life changing.

LIFE INVESTMENTS

So human flourishing, which arises out of our reflection of God's image, will always manifest itself as a commitment to relationship: relationship with God and relationship with each other. Any other priority will ultimately lead to dehumanization, to becoming less human. Jesus seems to warn about this possibility when he calls his disciples to be the salt of the earth. He says, "You are the salt of the earth. But if the salt loses its saltiness, how can it be made salty again? It is no longer good for anything, except to be thrown out and trampled underfoot."[12] Jesus cautions his followers not to lose their human flavor. When life becomes tasteless, it loses its purpose and its value. It can be easy to lose hope and doubt whether life is worth living.

In the previous chapter, we explored how our failure to value relationships is ultimately leading to a culture of death and not a culture of vibrant life. We are rejecting getting married and having families, and whole cultures are actually dying out. Or we are having kids but then regretting that choice when we see how much time and energy parenthood requires. We are rejecting deep friendships and instead dying alone in our apartments. Instead of talking to each other, we talk to robots and algorithms that we have designed to parrot what we think we want to hear. Instead of using social media to build meaningful connections with others, we too often use it to post curated snapshots of lives that don't actually exist. We obsess about the data of social media—the likes, follows, shares—in an effort to gain levels of attention that will satisfy us until our next post. We are taught to see ourselves as self-sufficient and beautiful, like Narcissus peering into the pool, and then are surprised that our loneliness is killing us.

What would our lives look like if, instead of following culture's lead, we followed Jesus' and believed what he said about what leads to human flourishing? It's interesting how much attention people will pay to how best to invest their money, but how little attention to how best to invest their lives. When I finished college and started working, I decided it was time to be responsible and invest for retirement. The only trouble is that I didn't know what I was doing. That first year was a crash course in learning that some investments are better than others. I've known people who have lost large amounts of money with poor investments or fallen prey to a ponzi scheme. But what's more devastating is seeing those who have made poor life investments. That some mutual funds lead to a better return than others is Finance 101, but have you ever considered that some time investments are more valuable than others?

Take a moment to consider your life and how you're investing your time. It reminds me of my friend Sheri, who helped me with this book. She loves to read more than anyone I know. She once told me that she keeps track of how many books she reads each month and each year. Some quick multiplication was all it took to calculate how many books she could expect to read in an average lifetime. It worked out to only a few thousand books that she'll be able to read this side of heaven. Finding this incredibly depressing, she began to reconsider what books are worth investing in. Was it worth slogging through a poorly written or boring book just to finish it, or should she be more willing to put it aside and dive into something more meaningful?

Our lives are like that, aren't they? I don't mean that we should just abandon everything hard or unpleasurable in life. Rather, I mean that we have only so many years to invest in things that really matter and our finite time on earth should cause us to choose carefully. Jesus also drives at this question, but from a slightly different angle, in Matthew chapter 6, saying, "For where your treasure is, there your heart will be also."[13] If you want to know what you love, look at what you're investing your life in. What do you spend your time and money on? Is it worth it? It's far too easy to squander your life.

I want to make it clear that choosing what matters and being committed to relationships doesn't mean that you have to be married to be a good Christian or that you have to have kids or that you have to be an extrovert. What it does mean is that your life will show a pattern of radical commitment to relationship in a way that is self-sacrificial. My mom has been a great example of this to me. When I was a kid, we were in church one day when the pastor mentioned that there was a need at a nursing home for people to visit the elderly. So the next week, my mom packed my siblings and me up and drove us to the nursing home, where we met a little old lady named Eloisa. She was eighty-six and had been a school teacher in her younger years. Her husband had passed away in 1962, and since then she had been all alone. So every week for the next six years, my mom brought us back to visit Eloisa. I remember running races down the halls with my sister and going from room to room to say hi to all the residents. The man in the room next to hers was named Lucky, and we often played cards with him. No one was ever annoyed that there were kids stampeding all over the nursing home. They so appreciated our willingness to have simple conversation that they accepted how loud and unruly we were. As I reflect on those years, I realize that Eloisa was investing in us as much as we were investing in her. It was time well spent.

BODYBUILDING WITH JESUS

So if we agree that the Bible teaches that relationship with God and relationship with others is the foundation for a life of flourishing, then it raises the question: What do flourishing lives look like?

After telling his disciples that they are to be the salt of the earth, Jesus spends the rest of the Sermon on the Mount teaching them what a truly flourishing human life looks like. The truth is, his description of a flourishing life doesn't look anything like what we would imagine.

Take a minute to think about your life. If you could imagine the best possible life for yourself, a life where you are truly thriving, what would that look like? For some, the word *thriving* conjures images of wealth: having a beautiful dream house or exciting vacations. For others, the idea of thriving involves health: finally being free of pain and sickness. For most everyone, thriving means pleasure and happiness: having a job that you enjoy, spending time with loved ones, feeling satisfaction and accomplishment at the end of the day.

But did any of your imaginings of a flourishing life include persecution? Jesus said that it might. He said, "Blessed are you when people insult you, persecute you and falsely say all kinds of evil against you because of me."[14] What about suffering? Jesus describes a life following him by saying, "If anyone slaps you on the right cheek, turn to them the other cheek also."[15] Did your image of thriving include loving your enemies or praying for those who persecute you?

Sometimes flourishing as God defines it does not look like flourishing to us. But that isn't because God is wrong. It's because we are. God alone can define flourishing because he created us and knows what is truly good. When God promises that following him will lead to flourishing, it's important to remember that he is less concerned about our temporary happiness and comfort here on earth than he is about our eternal good. In the West, there is this pervasive idea that we are living a good life if we are always comfortable or if we have no suffering at all. Christianity contests that idea. Flourishing to God doesn't just mean eighty years of relative tranquility and pleasure. It means real peace and joy starting now and continuing forever and ever with him. Understanding the difference between those ideas of flourishing requires a change in perspective.

Our perspective changes how we live. For example, when I was in college I worked odd jobs during the summer to make money. Some summer jobs were great, and others were terrible. My favorite summer job was building greeting-card stands in grocery stores. Three of my best friends were working with me, and we had a great summer that went by too quickly. However, the next summer I worked at a warehouse that was managed like an internment camp. That summer was a grind. Yet I didn't break down and throw in the towel because I knew that September was coming. Our flourishing depends on our perspective.

Similarly, when I was twelve, I had come to the conclusion that, in the face of death, life was meaningless. A few years later, I remember one day being in a serious existential crisis at school and asking my weightlifting teacher, "What's the purpose to all this?" I figured that he had more determination than anyone else I knew, so therefore he must have life figured out. I was genuinely seeking guidance. I'll never forget his puzzled look as he barked at me to hit the bench press. As I slid the weights onto the bar and began to lift, I realized that the motion of pushing the weights up and down had become a metaphor of life. I was lost in a sea of meaningless repetition in which suffering in the gym made no sense. Neither did suffering in schoolwork. I did the bare minimum to get through high school and that's it.

When I became a Christian at seventeen, I began to understand what Jesus offers, and my perspective changed. Eternity changes everything.

Consider weightlifting. We all understand that exercise has a purpose, to build muscle or get into shape, and some people, myself included, even find pleasure and satisfaction in lifting weights. However, the older you get, the more you realize that exercise is temporal. Sure, you can build a great bod now, but time will ultimately rob you of the gains you've made. Eventually you will get weak, need a cane or a wheelchair, get sick, and die like everybody else, and the muscles you worked so hard to hone will disappear. Given this reality, exercise can become depressing.

Without Jesus, life is like weightlifting. Without eternity, a life of flourishing can't possibly include suffering, because without eternity, suffering is meaningless. Yet when we realize that how we live in this life affects eternity, suddenly suffering becomes not only tolerable but also beautiful. Rather than being meaningless, suffering becomes infused with purpose and hope. God hasn't forgotten us in our suffering. He hasn't promised a life of flourishing and then reneged on us. Rather, he is using our sufferings for our present good and our eternal joy. The apostle Paul uses this thought to encourage the first-century Christians living in Rome, writing, "We boast in the hope of the glory of God. Not only so, but we also glory in our sufferings, because we know that suffering produces perseverance; perseverance, character; and character, hope."[16] Later on in his letter, he says, "I consider that our present sufferings are not worth comparing with the glory that will be revealed in us."[17]

Now, I don't want to talk about suffering and give you the idea that the Christian life, a life that God promised would be for our flourishing, is all heartache and adversity and pain. But it's important to make clear that flourishing doesn't mean a life without those things either. God told us that we were made to be together, to be in relationship with him and with each other, and the reality is that we aren't in the garden of Eden anymore. Being committed to loving God and loving others is going to mean some heartache, but it will also mean great joy.

I learned this firsthand while on a day hike with my family. As we came down the mountain, an icy cold wind caught us unprepared. My eleven-year-old son, Tristan, was shaking and struggling to keep his hands warm, so I asked if he wanted to wear my jacket. In typical Tristan fashion, he declined. He was going to tough it out. Instead of reasoning with him and convincing him to take my jacket, I just took it off and put it around him. I zipped the oversized jacket up and we continued down the mountain. After about thirty minutes, I asked if he was warmer. "Yes," he replied begrudgingly, "but I'm not happy about it!" "Why is that?" I asked. He responded, "I know I'm warm only because you're cold." He hadn't wanted to take my jacket because he knew that I would suffer. It's a feeling I could relate to. We don't like people suffering for us. But as a parent, I was happy to be cold for his sake. Yes, I suffered, but because I love him there was beauty in that suffering.

Now, I'm aware that my discomfort on that mountain was pretty minor in the scope of human suffering. Yet the idea that hope, love, meaning, and beauty can go hand in hand with suffering has been echoed in the lives of Christians for thousands of years. The presence of suffering is not a contradiction to a life of flourishing, and in some instances might even be a path to it. Read stories about missionaries, the persecuted church, and Christians in wars or concentration camps and you will hear these echoes. Read the apostle Paul's second letter to the church in Corinth. In chapter 12 he reminds the church that suffering is a good thing because it is only in our weakness that God's power can fill us up. He says, "That is why, for Christ's sake, I delight in weaknesses, in insults, in hardships, in persecutions, in difficulties. For when I am weak, then I am strong."[18]

Or just talk to Pastor Lee. Many people would look at his life and see only how painful it is, how much he has sacrificed. Certainly when I watched him hold that two-week-old baby and pray over him, there was grief there. Babies were not made to be abandoned. Yet look at the flourishing that Pastor Lee has brought to his own life and to the lives of those around him. Seoul is a richer, more loving, more human place because of his work. There are thousands of people who are alive because of Pastor Lee's commitment to believe Jesus and what he said leads to human flourishing. Jesus said that the best life is one in which we value relationships, with God and with others.

PART 4

HOW SHOULD HUMANS LIVE?

OF WEDDINGS AND
FUNERALS

The summer of 2001 ended with me staring out the large glass window of my parents' house. As I watched the wind blow through the tree branches, rustling the leaves, I pondered the biggest decision of my life. It was two weeks before I was to be married, and I had doubts.

This wasn't the first time I was unsure of our future together. One time, when Nancy and I had been dating for a while, I moved from Portland, Oregon, back up to Vancouver, British Columbia, in Canada and had to change my phone number. I didn't call her for two weeks. My doubts just wouldn't let me pick up the phone. Finally, Nancy decided she had waited long enough and called my mom to get my phone number. I'll never forget what she said when she called me. In a cool but confident tone she said, "Andy, if you want to break up with me, you'll need to do it like a man." The line went silent as she waited for my reply. Man, was she feisty, and I needed it! Her love for me was unwavering, but she also wasn't about to let herself get pushed around. I loved Nancy, but I was terrified of marriage, and she knew it.

Eventually I built up the courage to ask her to marry me, but now here I was again rethinking our relationship. I loved my fiancée, but I was captured by the fear that I was making the wrong choice, or even worse, that she was. I had seen so many marriages end in divorce, including my own parents'. I wasn't confident that I would be a good husband, and I worried that she was making the wrong choice by marrying me. That day as I stared out the window, I knew that whatever I decided would direct the course of my entire life.

That afternoon, I called up my friend Darren, who lived in Montana, and asked if I could come stay with him for a while. Confused, he said, "Andy, I'm about to come out to Vancouver for your wedding." I explained that I was going to call off the wedding. He was surprised but assured me that I always had a place to stay with him. Then, half joking, he asked, "Can I have a shot with her?" Of course, I wanted to slug him. Yet I also couldn't blame him. My friend thought Nancy was wonderful, and he was right! That's what made everything so difficult. It was really about me and not her. Over the next two days, as I prepared to call off the wedding, I just couldn't do it. The thought of missing out on a life with Nancy, or watching someone else have a life with her, was unbearable. So on September 9, 2001, we stood before God, family, and friends and vowed our lives to each other in marriage.

During the ceremony, as Nancy and I held hands and looked deeply into each other's eyes, our pastor, Lorin Fischer, began to read these words from the Bible: "Even though I walk through the valley of the shadow of death, I will fear no evil."[1] Yep— apparently he had decided that the best topics for our wedding were fear, evil, and death. I remember thinking, "He knows this is a wedding and not a funeral, right?" Sure, he was old, but not *that* old. That's when I realized that he had deliberately chosen this passage, and I remember thinking that maybe this whole marriage thing was even more intense than I had imagined!

The truth is, Pastor Fischer was right—there is plenty to fear in life, and marriage is no exception. There is the fear of giving your love away to someone who might misuse it, but also the fear of losing that love, especially in death. After the sermon, it was time for our vows. I was nervous but excited to read the vows I had written for Nancy. Yet as I read my heartfelt promises to her, that nagging doubt prickled in the back of my mind. Could I really do this? Like most vows, ours were full of romantic and idealistic promises that I desperately wanted to keep but, at the same time, knew that I couldn't completely. My vows to Nancy included these promises: "You will be able to count on me in your times of joy and laughter, tears and sorrow. My ears will always be attentive when you need to talk. It will be my pleasure to always make time for you. I will seek your best interest with an attitude of patience, kindness, and respect."

If you're wondering how I still know these lines, word for word, it's because Pastor Fischer had both of our vows engraved onto a wooden plaque that hangs on the wall in our bedroom. He probably thought I would enjoy a constant reminder of my shortcomings, because—no surprise—we haven't always lived up to those vows. There have been plenty of times we have failed to listen and make time for each other. We have lost our patience and been unkind.

I'LL TRY TO LOVE YOU

Despite how desperately I wanted to love like that, I knew that I wouldn't be able to fulfill my vows the very moment that I said them. So should I not have made those vows? Should I have sprinkled in some disclaimers? Maybe I should have said, "My ears will always be attentive when you need to talk, unless it's going to make me late for work or my TV show is just getting to the good part."

Of course not! Just because we know that we can never live up to the ideal doesn't mean that we shouldn't have an ideal in the first place. After all, that's how a country works, isn't it?

A democratic state isn't so different from a marriage. It's a group of people who freely join together and uphold a set of ideals or standards. But in the case of a country, we call those standards laws instead of vows. Everyone knows that sometimes those laws will be broken. That's why we have police and prisons. The inevitability of broken laws doesn't render the laws pointless. It makes them essential.

The preamble to the Constitution of the United States says, "We hold these truths to be self-evident, that all men are created equal, that they are endowed by their Creator with certain unalienable Rights, that among these are Life, Liberty and the pursuit of Happiness." The Constitution claims that everyone naturally knows what the standard for a good country is. Likewise, in all my years of officiating weddings, I've never had a couple confused on what to vow to each other. Should I promise love or selfishness? Should I promise compassion or anger? Faithfulness or infidelity? No one asks those questions. Each couple may fret over the exact word choice, but all of them intuitively understand the broad strokes of what a good relationship looks like.

I think the same can be said of morality. When citizens uphold the basic laws of a country as self-evident, they are really acknowledging that a standard of morality exists. Likewise, the fact that people in love feel compelled to make grandiose vows to each other is evidence that a standard of relationship actually exists. The fact that people break laws and forsake their vows doesn't negate the existence of morality but rather upholds it. After all, divorce shouldn't hurt if we weren't meant to be faithful in the first place. Lying and cruelty shouldn't cause pain if we weren't meant to be honest and kind. Failure to live up to an ideal doesn't mean the ideal is broken. It means we are.

Our culture has a strange relationship with the idea of universal morality. Our culture has denied God's existence, removed him from every sphere of life, and then ridiculed those who believe otherwise. Yet when we erased God, we necessarily eroded the foundation for morality and thus erased part of what it means to be human.

Morality is essential to humanity. Even Charles Darwin argued that it is *the* key ingredient to being human. In *The Descent of Man,* he says, "I fully subscribe to the judgment of those writers . . . who maintain that of all the differences between man and the lower animals, the moral sense or conscience is by far the most important . . . it is summed up in that short but imperious word 'ought,' so full of high significance. It is the most noble of all the attributes of man."[2]

Even atheist psychologist and popular author Steven Pinker agrees about the importance of morality to our concept of being human. He writes, "Morality is not just any old topic in psychology but close to our conception of the meaning of life. Moral goodness is what gives each of us the sense that we are worthy human beings."[3] So when we ask the question of what it means to be human, it is unavoidable: we must consider morality, *how* humans should live.

It's no coincidence that the removal of God from our culture has been accompanied by a growing moral relativism. What's right is what's right for you. Anything is fine, as long as it doesn't hurt anyone else. Live *your* truth. You do you. Those are the maxims Western culture has embraced. That's because without God, there is no such thing as good and evil, right and wrong, at least not universally. In the absence of divine authority, morality can only be culturally constructed, which means that it can't possibly be for all people for all time. Yet what's ironic is that this same culture that denies objective moral values, that rejects real truth, also has a very strong idea of what is right and what is not. Our culture is full of social-justice warriors who use "Justice!" as a battle cry for all sorts of causes, not realizing that without God, there is no such thing. Our culture rejects God's definition of good and evil but then gets angry at God for the existence of evil and, ironically, uses it as an excuse not to believe in him, never realizing that without God, nothing can even be called evil in the first place.

WHODUNNIT?

I saw a clear example of this irony when I read a book by atheist author Sam Harris called *Letter to a Christian Nation*. In the book, he questions the goodness of God, asking why God would allow the murder of good people if he really loved them. Harris posits a realistic scenario: "Somewhere in the world a man has abducted a little girl. Soon he will rape, torture, and kill her. If an atrocity of this kind is not occurring at precisely this moment, it will happen in a few hours, or days at most."[4] Assuming that this child's parents believe in an all-powerful and all-loving God, Harris asks, "Are they right to believe this? Is it *good* that they believe this? No. The entirety of atheism is contained in this response." It's clear from his outrage that Sam Harris believes that kidnapping, rape, torture, and murder are wrong. I agree. I know those things are evil because they go against the nature of God. But Sam Harris doesn't believe in God. How, then, does he know those things are wrong?

Six years after *Letter to a Christian Nation,* Harris wrote a book detailing the implications of his godless worldview called *Free Will*. In it, he writes, "Free will *is* an illusion. Our wills are simply not of our own making. Thoughts and intentions emerge from background causes of which we are unaware and over which we exert no conscious control."[5] The reason for this, he explains, is that "my mental life is simply given to me by the cosmos." In a world without God, we are ruled by the background causes of physical laws and circumstances. Yet the problem is that morality requires free will. It can't be said that you ought to do one thing unless it was possible for you not to do it. That's why we don't condemn rocks as evil after a rockslide. They didn't freely decide to fall down the mountain. They were compelled by physical laws and couldn't resist. Thus, a rockslide isn't a moral problem. When Sam Harris decided that free will is an illusion, if we can say that he truly decided it at all, he likewise confirmed that morality is also an illusion.

With that in mind, let's go back to his problem about the man who kidnaps a little girl. If humankind has no free will, why is he so angry about this man's actions? Could that man have done otherwise? Certainly not, if he has no control over his thoughts and intentions. How, then, can we really blame him? Further, how can we really blame God?

As we saw in chapter 2, the idea of a purely physical world without God goes back to the Greeks and has only recently come back into popularity. In the nineteenth century, a French thinker named Pierre-Simon Laplace took this kind of thinking to its natural conclusion. Based on the cause-and-effect relationship in Newtonian physics, he argued that it is theoretically possible to calculate the trajectory and velocity of every single particle in the universe, every atom and molecule, including those that make up humans.[6] In so doing, it would be possible to know exactly where each part is coming from and where each one is going. According to this view, when the universe exploded into existence, it set off a chain reaction of events. Once the first domino was toppled, each other domino would necessarily fall, one after the other, in a perfectly predictable pattern. Accordingly, our lives are not free but instead are held captive to the push and pull of nature's laws. This view of the world is called causal determinism. It's the idea that everything in our lives was determined to take place from the beginning of the universe and we are just along for the ride.

Determinism in its original form has been challenged by the advent of quantum mechanics. When exploring extremely small objects, like subatomic particles, scientists found that the laws of Newtonian physics didn't apply. Rather than following a set of rules, subatomic particles seem to behave randomly. Initially, this discovery appeared to undermine the deterministic position. How can everything be determined if the smallest bits, like a quark or a photon, behave randomly? However, as scientists studied, they realized that while individual subatomic particles seem to behave randomly, collectively they average out and form consistent and predictable patterns. For this reason, for larger objects, determinism is still held to be true.

How randomness and determinism blend is always being debated. However, it doesn't matter. The most important thing to realize is that when it comes to morality, a determined universe is ultimately the same thing as a random universe. They are two sides of the same coin. In either case, humans are reduced to puppets. Whether I did something because my atoms were determined to do it or because my atoms randomly did it doesn't really matter. In either case, *I* didn't do it and so I can't really be blamed for my actions, can I? In both cases, we don't actually exist as free persons able to make decisions but instead are slaves to the cosmos. Ultimately, I am absolved of responsibility for my actions, and thus I cannot be good or evil or make decisions based on love or hate.

Doesn't it seem a little odd that if free will and morality are illusions, it is possible for us to become aware of the illusions? Further, if it is indeed correct that everything is determined, how could anyone ever know whether determinism is true or false? After all, you believe only what you were determined to believe, including that determinism is true. If another person believes that determinism is false, they were determined to believe that. In that case, what is an illusion and what is truth?

Ironically, people often attempt to prove determinism is true with science.

Yet the real irony of using science to prove determinism is that science requires freedom in the first place. Science is an act of curiosity, learning, and discovery that fundamentally requires that we have the ability to search for truth and find it. After all, science is possible only if I can trust that my five senses give me an accurate representation of the world and if my mind has the freedom to draw correct conclusions from this information.

Consider what science was like in Russia under the rule of Joseph Stalin.[7] In the 1930s, Stalin began supporting a man named Trofim Lysenko, who rejected the normal understanding of genetics. Lysenko's mistaken beliefs conveniently coincided with communist ideologies, and so Stalin made Lysenko's theories law in Russia. He threw those scientists who disagreed with him into prison, even killing some of them, and began dictating what scientists could study and what conclusions they had to draw from their research. The result was not real science at all but pseudoscience. Real science requires the freedom to draw conclusions from evidence, even if those conclusions disagree with what the government, other scientists, or the prevailing culture wants to hear. Lysenko's bogus beliefs about genetics stalled agricultural research in Russia for decades, contributed to widespread crop failure, and condemned millions to die of famine.

Determinism handcuffs science the same way that Joseph Stalin did. With determinism, nothing I believe about the world is true because it is objectively true. It is true only because my unconscious brain was determined to have that belief. Arguably, since the Big Bang, the atoms in my brain have predecided what I study and even what conclusions I draw. How can the result be any different than the pseudoscience of Russia? Likewise, how can we condemn Stalin for taking away the freedom of Russians? According to determinism, they never had any freedom to begin with. Determinism always brings us back to those tricky questions: What is truth? What is an illusion? How can we tell the difference?

LOVESICK ATHEIST

A chance to explore these ideas presented itself to me one day in the form of a young adult named Ryan who showed up in my church's office looking to talk with a pastor. As I often do, I invited Ryan to join me for a walk around our church property to get some exercise and talk about what was on his mind. As we walked, Ryan told me he was an atheist. Naturally, I anticipated that he wanted to talk about the existence of God. To my surprise, he actually wanted to talk about his love life. In high school, Ryan had fallen in love with a girl and they had begun to date. Soon after they graduated, his girlfriend had become a Christian. After wrestling with the decision for some time, she broke up with him because of their increasingly opposed worldviews.

As we talked it became clear what Ryan was really after: he wanted me to back him up and convince this ex-girlfriend that they should get back together. Instead, I asked Ryan a question: "Why are you so upset about this breakup?" He told me how much he loved this girl and how he had hoped to marry her one day. I then asked, "Ryan, what do you mean by love? According to your worldview, isn't love just some chemical reactions in your brain?" As we began to make another lap around the church, Ryan looked down at the asphalt and thought about my question. Stopping in the parking lot, he responded, "Yeah, I guess that's what I believe." "Perfect!" I declared joyfully. "Just go duplicate that chemical reaction with someone else."

Ryan paused and cocked his head and said, "But I don't want to." "Why?" I asked. "What's so special about your chemical reactions with this particular girl? There're plenty of other ways for your brain to get a hit of dopamine."

That day as we walked laps around the church, I explained to Ryan that I thought he was cheating on his worldview. He clearly understood that the love he was experiencing was more than just chemicals in the brain. He was only paying lip service to a worldview, not wanting to live as though it were true. I didn't convince Ryan out of his atheism that day, but I did give him something to think about.

Could you imagine what marriage vows would sound like if people lived out what Ryan claimed to believe? Could you imagine saying "I do" to this: "Currently, the chemical reactions in my amygdala make me feel like I love you. Here's to hoping those reactions continue. At least I can promise that I will always forgive you, because I know that free will is an illusion and thus you aren't responsible for your actions. I don't really know the predetermined trajectories of my atoms, but I hope that they will always keep me by your side"? If someone had the courage to read such nonsense during their vows, I think the whole crowd would burst out laughing. The very idea would be hilarious if not for the great number of people who believe those words are true.

Philosopher David Johnson illustrates this nonsense by explaining how he is forced to live in a way that is inconsistent with his own worldview. During his lecture on why free will does not exist, he concludes with surprising honesty, saying,

> I'll admit it. I find the arguments against free will quite
> persuasive. Philosophically, I think it is undeniable that
> humans do not possess free will . . . However, when I'm not
> thinking about philosophy, when I'm out living my daily

life—hell, even when I am thinking about philosophy—I still think I'm making free decisions. It still seems to me that I have free will. I can't help but believe I do. I even feel like I'm making free decisions right now about what words to say. I can even choose some random nonsense thing to say, "Uh gibbildy-goo." It really seems like I freely chose to say "gibbildy-goo." I can't deny the feeling, and even the belief that I am free, regardless of how philosophically I am convinced that I am not.[8]

Intuitively, Johnson knows that his worldview is unlivable. Despite how much he may want to, he can't actually live his life as though what he believes is true. Yet rather than consider the simpler alternative—that maybe he feels free because he is—he makes peace with his cognitive dissonance by suggesting that he feels free because he was determined to, even though he somehow knows that it is a lie.

This might sound like philosophical nonsense—thought experiments that don't impact daily life. Yet the truth is that our beliefs about determinism and free will directly impact our understanding of who we are as humans and how we should live. Remember, if people are not responsible for their actions, then they are also not morally culpable for them. There is no right and wrong.

The implications of this kind of thinking are horrifying. In an *Atlantic* article about free will, philosopher and writer Stephen Cave lists multiple studies that show how our beliefs about free will shape our behavior. Unsurprisingly, holding a deterministic worldview can make people worse employees and students, make them less compassionate and generous, and cause them to doubt the meaning of life. He writes, "The list goes on: Believing that free will is an illusion has been shown to make people less creative, more likely to conform, less willing to learn from their mistakes, and less grateful toward one another. In every regard, it seems, when we embrace determinism, we indulge our dark side."[9]

David Johnson goes a step farther and suggests that a scientific rejection of free will should change how we handle the prison system. He says, "Regardless of how free we feel, and even how we feel about those that commit crimes, an argument that criminals freely choose to do their crimes, and are thus morally responsible, would have no legs to stand on. Even if we can't help but feel hatred towards a serial killer, we will not be justified locking him away on moral grounds."[10]

If this is the case, then jails are not at all about justice. Rather than rightly punishing people for their immoral actions, jails become purely human zoos. We don't keep tigers behind bars because their carnivorism is morally wrong but because we are worried that they will eat us. Likewise, Johnson's argument implies, we shouldn't keep child rapists behind bars because their actions are morally wrong but because we are worried they will rape our children. It's purely a question of safety, not right and wrong.

Do we really believe that? I wish that Sam Harris and David Johnson were just rare exceptions to common sense, but they're not. Many in academia embrace and teach varying degrees of determinism to university students across the world. What would happen if those students started to act like it was true?

KILLER EDUCATION

Sadly, in 1924, two students did act on what they were reading in university. Newspapers at the time called it "the crime of the century," and it's best that we don't forget it.[11] On May 22, 1924, a fourteen-year-old boy named Bobby Franks vanished from the streets of Chicago. Shortly after his disappearance, a ransom note was delivered to the Franks family demanding ten thousand dollars. Yet before his parents could deliver the money, Bobby's naked body was found on the outskirts of town. His killers had poured acid on his face and genitals to conceal their crime. There was even talk that Bobby had been raped.

The murder of Bobby Franks was a terrible crime, reminiscent of the hypothetical one that Sam Harris proposed. On the one hand is the idea that a good God allowed a terrible evil to take place and that one day he will deliver judgment for it, and on the other hand is the belief that there is no God, just deterministic forces, and thus there is no good or evil and no judgment is required. Take your pick.

As the case developed and the details emerged, the murder grew in notoriety. What made this case so noteworthy was not just the heinous crime that was committed but also the philosophical motives behind the murder and the perpetrators' defense. After much careful planning, eighteen-year-old Nathan Leopold and nineteen-year-old Richard Loeb had set out to commit the perfect crime. Their intent was to abduct someone, collect a ransom, and then murder them without getting caught.

They planned to tie a rope around their victim's neck and together pull at either end of the cord until the victim suffocated to death. In this way, they could both share in the experience of murder and be equally responsible. It was by chance that day that they came across Bobby, whom Loeb was related to and knew well. It didn't take much to convince Bobby to get into their car. When he sat down in the front seat, Leopold reached over from the back seat and hit him on the head with a chisel. They placed a gag into Bobby's mouth. However, before they could carry out the rest of their evil plan, they discovered that the gag had suffocated Bobby. So they changed plans, stripped off the boy's clothes, poured acid on him, and dumped the body.

Although Bobby was already dead, Leopold and Loeb still

went through with demanding a ransom. Neither Leopold nor Loeb was motivated by money, as they both came from wealthy families. They merely wanted the challenge of collecting a ransom without getting caught. Yet in the end, the ransom note and the clues left at the scene led to their arrest.

During the highly publicized trial that followed their capture, it became clear that both Leopold and Loeb were highly intelligent and that together they made a deadly combination. Loeb was obsessed with crime and Leopold was obsessed with Friedrich Nietzsche. Nietzsche, as we discussed in chapter 2, was the nineteenth-century philosopher who famously declared the death of God. He believed that a universe without God was a world without purpose, value, or morality. This view of the world is summed up in the term *nihilism.*

Nietzsche believed that the path to nihilism lay in rising above the religious superstition of morality to see what others could not—that there is no right or wrong. Those capable of breaking free from this illusion of morality could become their own god—an *Übermensch,* meaning above-human or superhuman. Leopold was convinced by Nietzsche's philosophy and understood that he was one of these superhumans. In turn, he convinced Loeb to accept it as well. They believed that their superior intellect allowed them to rise above the moral rules that held captive the feebleminded. In this way, they dehumanized Bobby and paved the way to murder him. Leopold and Loeb thought that they were free to decide for themselves how they should live. Murder, they decided, was an acceptable action for them so long as it gave them pleasure.

Many people today agree with Leopold and Loeb, believing that pleasure is the primary guiding principle for how humans should live. In 2012, Starbucks teamed up with Oprah to give some sage advice on their coffee sleeves. One cup of coffee I bought said, "Follow your passion. It will lead to your purpose."

Another one said, "The only courage you ever need is the courage to live the life you want." I can imagine Leopold and Loeb wholeheartedly agreeing with those sentiments as they went searching for their victim.

We can all think of passions that some consider pleasurable and yet that society rightly condemns. Rape, pedophilia, murder—those are real pleasures for some people. Yet in those cases, nobody would suggest they follow Oprah's advice and find the courage to live the life they want. Likewise, Leopold and Loeb had a passion for breaking the law. Over time they had slowly worked their way from petty theft to murder. In court they explained that their desire to murder the boy was partly for the thrill of it and partly as a scientific experiment. They wanted to know what the experience of murder was like. Clearly, pleasure or passion alone can't determine how humans should live.

Leopold and Loeb's defense lawyer was Clarence Darrow, who later also served as a defense lawyer at the Scopes Monkey Trial. Considering that Leopold and Loeb were both guilty, that they had boasted to others of their crime, and that throughout the trial they showed no remorse, Darrow had his work cut out for him. His goal was to cast doubt on whether the boys were truly reponsible for their actions. He did this by appealing to those old standbys determinism and randomness. In his closing argument, he said, "I know, Your Honor, that every atom of life in all this universe is bound up together. I know that a pebble cannot be thrown into the ocean without disturbing every drop of water in the sea . . . I know that all life is a series of infinite chances, which sometimes result one way and sometimes another . . . Why should this boy's life be bound up with Frederick Nietzsche, who died thirty years ago, insane, in Germany? I don't know. I only know it is."[12]

Darrow argued that people are no more capable of free will

than a machine following its design or an insect following its instinct. He concluded that crime was not a choice and thus Leopold and Loeb should not be punished for murdering Bobby Franks. In the end, Darrow's argument was successful enough to stave off the death penalty. Both Leopold and Loeb were given life sentences in prison.

MORAL FACTS AND WINE

The story of Leopold and Loeb continues to raise one of the most important questions of our time: Are people governed only by natural laws, or are we also accountable to a moral law that guides and directs how humans should live?

A world without God and without free will naturally leads to a world composed of natural laws and devoid of moral responsibility. Some have tried to rectify this problem with some fancy philosophical footwork: What if moral laws just exist as part of the universe, like physical laws do? Or in a similar vein, some propose that perhaps moral laws arose hand in hand with human evolution. According to that argument, moral laws are natural byproducts of intelligence, and all behaviors that we see as moral can be traced back to behaviors that were helpful for the success of the human species. Either way, whether the moral law arose as a part of our evolution or just exists as a fact of the universe, we wouldn't need God in order to keep morality.

I heard this argument while in Wisconsin for a conference. I was sitting at a table sipping a glass of red wine and talking philosophy and theology with a friend when a PhD student from Colorado joined us. The young student had a name tag that said Jeff, and he quietly listened in on our conversation. As soon as the conversation turned to morality, he jumped in. Quickly, it became apparent that Jeff did not share our worldview. I was discussing the need for God in order for morality to make sense, but Jeff disagreed. He was an atheist but hadn't swallowed the poison of Nietzsche's nihilism. Instead, he insisted that morality does exist and that it is binding on all people. My friend and I were both intrigued and began to question his view. Jeff argued that morality is a fact of the universe, like any other fact such as gravity or mathematics. He didn't attempt to explain where it came from or how we are aware of it. He just stated that it exists and that all humans know it. It's an interesting idea and I'm glad he believes morality does exist, but without God his position has some major flaws.

First, even if morality does exist as facts, how could we ever truly know those facts? You'll remember that this idea of knowledge was also a problem when we looked at determinism. If determinism is true, we could never really know that it is true, since whether we believe or don't believe in determinism is not a free choice based on evidence but only what the universe determined that we would believe. Likewise, because moral facts don't assert themselves in the same way that physical laws do, how do we go about discovering these moral facts? Through group consensus? That seems unreliable. Consensus has come to some terrible conclusions about what is right and wrong in cultures across the globe. Through our own opinions? Again, that seems unreliable, especially when we remember people like Leopold and Loeb. Are these moral facts testable and repeatable like physical laws are?

Second, the existence of a moral law does not mean that I have to abide by it. Moral laws are different from natural laws because they allow for choices. I do not have a choice about whether to abide by gravity. I might decide that gravity is nonsense and jump off the roof of my house so I can fly like a bird, but I will quickly find that denying natural laws comes with consequences. With moral laws, though, that moment of truth doesn't necessarily come. If there is no God and this life on earth is all there is, then there is no reason why I can't or shouldn't choose to act against a moral fact and get away with it. Yes, we might argue that eventually it will come back to bite you, that justice will prevail, and that all evildoers will get their just deserts. But without God, is that true? Not necessarily. Some thieves get caught and put in prison and some thieves just get really rich. If the moral law exists only as a fact, it certainly doesn't force me to listen. Likewise, if the moral law arose by natural selection to benefit the human species, then in our modern time shouldn't there be instances when we can ignore it? Can't we collectively ignore our instinct not to murder if murdering benefits the human genetic pool? The Nazis said yes. Without God, how can we say they were wrong?

Last, and most important, the existence of a moral law not only doesn't mean I have to abide by it but also doesn't mean that I should. When we use the word *duty,* we mean the obligations or responsibilities that we owe to other people, but that we never owe to objects. For example, I don't and can't owe my table anything. If I take a hot pan out of the oven for my dinner and place it directly down on my wooden table, it is going to burn and leave a mark. I might be disappointed, kicking myself for the mistake, but I wouldn't have disappointed the table itself, because I didn't owe anything to the table and I don't have a duty to protect it. On the other hand, if my wife was sitting at the table and I placed the hot pan right down on her lap, that is different. When I see her sitting there, I am aware that I have obligations to her in light of her humanity and our marriage that do not exist between me and the table. I have a duty not to hurt her.

In philosophy, the relationship I have with other people, such as my wife, are called I-Thou relationships. The relationship I have to objects, facts, or other nonpersons, such as my table, are referred to as I-It relationships. Only I-Thou relationships,

relationships with other people, invoke a sense of duty. When thinking about the moral law, then, what would my relationship to that moral law be? Is the law itself a person, an I-Thou relationship that I have an obligation to? No. Moral facts as Jeff envisioned them could only be considered an I-It relationship, and thus my relationship to them can only ever be akin to my relationship to a table. For example, if I steal from my neighbor, my obligation is to repay *him*, not to repay the moral fact itself. After all, it is only people, not facts, that can be wronged.

This is what makes the Christian understanding of morality so compelling. In Christianity, morality is not a fact. It is a person—God. Morality or right relationship flows from God's character. For this reason, I have an I-Thou relationship with morality, and thus I have a duty to treat God in a certain way. Likewise, because God made humans in his image, we have I-Thou relationships with each other. Those relationships put me in contact with persons who have inherent dignity and value. This goes back to what I said at the beginning of this book. When I see people correctly, I will treat them correctly.

Viktor Frankl, a psychiatrist and Jew who survived the German concentration camps of World War II, made this point back in 1946. In his book *Man's Search for Meaning,* he writes, "Freedom, however, is not the last word. Freedom is only part of the story and half of the truth. Freedom is but the negative aspect of the whole phenomenon whose positive aspect is responsibleness. In fact, freedom is in danger of degenerating into mere arbitrariness unless it is lived in terms of responsibleness. That is why *I recommend that the Statue of Liberty on the East Coast be supplemented by a Statue of Responsibility on the West Coast.*"[13]

Frankl's right. Freedom alone is not good. People can use their freedom for good or for evil. Freedom requires responsibility, and people are accountable for how they use it. But that's the issue. To whom is humanity responsible? How should humans live? Maybe a second statue would help us remember that freedom and responsibility necessarily go hand in hand. In essence, that's what morality is: the freedom to act and the responsibility to be accountable for those actions.

Christianity teaches that people are morally responsible to God. When we sin, we aren't seeing the truth of God and others correctly but instead are distorting them to I-It relationships. We dehumanize ourselves and each other, seeing humans as objects and treating them accordingly. Only with God can we treat each other like humans. Only with God can we know that our relationships, as illustrated in wedding vows, point to a relational standard greater than our ability to fulfill.

SKULL AND CROSSBONES

It was a cold, bleak November night the first time I went to prison. The outside walls stretched high, with barbed wire coiled at the top. Guards stood in watchtowers with spotlights monitoring from above while more armed guards circled the perimeter in vans. I was buzzed through thick metal doors which slammed shut behind me. They don't call it maximum security for nothing.

Thankfully, I wasn't there as a prisoner. I had been invited to speak to the inmates about a topic from my recent book, *Thinking?*[1] It was my first time addressing inmates, so beforehand I met up with the prison chaplain in a small diner nearby. This was actually our second attempt to get into the prison. A few weeks prior, I had been on my way when the prison suddenly went into lockdown. Apparently, something had gone missing that could be used as a weapon. All the inmates were locked in their cells so that guards could systematically search for the missing item. The lockdown lasted for days. This time I was hopeful that we could get in, but as I was buzzed through door after door, it began to feel like an odd thing to hope for.

Although these men had committed some grizzly crimes, I was assured that I would be relatively safe. As we went through security, I was searched, signed in, and given a special button that clipped onto my shirt. I was told that if anything got out of control, I was to push the button and armed guards would rush to my aid within seconds.

As we walked down the empty corridor to the room where I would be speaking, I realized just how grim and oppressive a maximum-security prison is. A building designed to isolate people and remove human freedom is a dark place to be. Arriving at the empty room, I looked around and waited for the inmates to be released from their cells one at a time. The chaplain introduced me to a few of the men as they came in. I found it difficult at first to know what to talk about. So much of our daily chitchat implies a level of freedom that was absent from their lives. Topics like how your job is going, your weekend plans, or even the weather don't go over so well in the slammer.

Then John walked in. It was like someone had turned on a light in a very dark room. I could tell immediately that this guy was different, and the chaplain was excited to introduce us. John was intimidatingly tall with a muscular build and a thick black beard. Although he was a massive figure, he had a contagious smile and joy that radiated against the gloomy backdrop of that prison. John stood out, and it was clear that the other inmates had a deep respect for him. Later, the only man I met who was scheduled to be released told me that John had changed his life by introducing him to Jesus. Only Jesus, he believed, could give him the hope he desperately needed and keep him from returning to jail.

John shook my hand, told me that he also loved Jesus and that he was thankful that I had come, even after the lockdown. As we talked, I learned that John was enrolled in an online Bible college, where he took one class at a time. I asked him who his favorite theologian was. He didn't hesitate: F. F. Bruce was his favorite and he was reading Bruce's book *Paul: Apostle of the Heart Set Free.* John told me that he loved his classes so much that he read every assigned book three times. The first read-through was quick and for enjoyment. The second was moderately paced so he could highlight the book's key ideas. The final reading was slow and thoughtful, as he took notes and contributed his own thoughts on the content. Remembering this description of his reading process makes me laugh now. I have spoken at numerous conferences and universities over the years, yet all of the best and most difficult questions I have received have come from inmates. After all, they do have a lot of time to read and think.

My conversation with John was cut short because it was time for my talk to begin. I was supposed to be addressing one of life's toughest topics: God and the existence of evil. As I stared at my audience, I questioned why I had agreed to this.

GUILTY AS CHARGED

Normally, when I speak on the subject of evil, I spend time explaining the horrible things that people have done to each other in order to convince my audience that evil is real and terrible. I realized that wasn't going to be necessary this time. These men were some of society's worst offenders. They knew evil exists because they had been its instrument and, interestingly, they weren't proud of it. The chaplain had warned me ahead of time not to ask the inmates what they had done. It's a source of incredible shame for these men and something they share only with those they trust. This shouldn't be all that surprising. Think about the worst thing you've ever done or thought. How willing would you be to share those details? It can take months, even years, for an inmate to open up to the chaplain about their crime, if ever.

I witnessed that shame firsthand at the end of the night when during the Q&A a man opened up about his crime. As I asked for questions, a middle-aged man stood up, stared at the ground, and then asked a question that I will never forget. Fighting back tears and in a shaky voice, he asked, "Why did God allow me to kill three people?" He then, slowly, sat back down.

I couldn't believe his courage and vulnerability. With everyone waiting for my response, I looked around and noticed that the guards and the chaplain were nowhere in sight. It was just me and around twenty inmates, who were waiting for an answer to one of life's most difficult questions. Unsure if he would like my answer, I had a keen awareness of the safety button clipped to my shirt. I was also comforted that John, the biggest guy in the room, was sitting in the front row, all smiles, vigorously taking notes.

Normally, when people bring up this topic, they ask why God allows evil. It's a far easier question to ask than why God allows *me* to do evil. We like to speak of evil as something that we experience as its victims, not as something we are guilty of as its participants. That's what makes removing God from our worldview both convenient and contradictory. Without God we are no longer responsible for evil, as we saw in the last chapter, but this is only because without God there is no such thing as good and evil or moral responsibility. Without God we are just mechanical slaves to the push and pull of the cosmos. Yet despite a worldview that denies moral responsibility, people continue to be repulsed by the evil of this world and want to hold someone responsible. That someone is often God. Instead of taking responsibility ourselves, we cast blame on a God we claim we don't believe in.

If we are to see ourselves and others as wholly human with the freedom to do good or evil, we are required first to see God. When we return God to our worldview, the universe changes. Instead of just a determined or random collection of parts, humanity, and indeed the universe, becomes a purposeful whole. Throughout this book, I have sought to show that humanity was created for the purpose of relationship and that this purpose defines our identity, our value, and what leads to our flourishing. In this last chapter, it's important to understand that we have been created for a specific kind of relationship. It's not enough just to have relationships; we also need to know how we should live in order for those relationships to flourish.

A GARDEN OF CHOICES

In discussing evil and how humans should live, it's helpful to go back to the very beginning, before there was evil, to see how humans lived then. The book of Genesis explains that God created the heavens and the earth and that the centerpiece of that creation was a garden, the garden of Eden. It was a utopian paradise where the first humans, Adam and Eve, lived in a right and good relationship with God and each other. The garden of Eden was beautiful, filled with trees and rivers and abundant food to eat. When God put humans there, he gave them meaningful work taking care of all the plants and animals in the garden. There was no evil there, no shame, no guilt. In every way, life in the garden was perfect.

What was it about the garden of Eden that made it so perfect? It's a pivotal question for understanding how humans should live, because what we believe about human flourishing will guide how we choose to live. In a sense, we are all trying to get back to the garden, to reach our own idea of the perfect life. In that quest, our culture offers a variety of paradise narratives, each saying something specific about what paradise looks like and thus how humans should live.

For a long time, humanity thought utopia would be found in the harvesting of the garden. After all, humans were told to work the garden; therefore the results of that work, the literal fruit of our labors, must be the important part. According to this view, paradise is what you can achieve and reap from the garden before you die. In this garden, people will cultivate the earth through whatever means are necessary to achieve the greatest yield. For Leopold II, that meant enslaving the Congolese, killing elephants for ivory, and purging the land of its most valuable resources. These days, capitalism has replaced slavery as the order of the day, but the goal is essentially the same: bigger, better, faster, stronger, higher, richer. Paradise to many means "more." The idea of *carpe diem*, or YOLO, as we phrased it in the 2010s, to some extent hinges on paradise being about harvesting the garden. Get what you can while you can. The goal of life, according to this view, is to use the time you have to increase—to get more stuff, more experiences, and ultimately more pleasure—and when you die, others will take what you have and try to do the same, *ad nauseam*.

Unsurprisingly, the greed inherent in this version of utopia has made some humans pause. Surely the solution to achieving paradise is not harvesting the garden to the point of destruction, right? Thus, many people have shifted their view away from the fruit of the garden and focused it on the garden itself. To them, paradise is not about harvesting the garden so much as it is about regrowing the garden. We've all seen captivating documentaries of the incredible beauty of our planet. From snowcapped mountains to deep blue oceans, there is no question that both the planet and the incredible diversity of plants and animals are spectacular. Yet those same documentaries seek to point out how we are ruining this planet by polluting its air, soil, and water. We have left the oceans empty of life but filled with our garbage, and the land has become permanently scarred by our plundering. In light of this bleak outlook, for many people, paradise means reversing the devastation by regrowing a pristine and sustainable earth unmarred by the effects of human greed. Environmentalism and extreme animal activism, like the kind discussed in chapter 3, are movements that have grown from this understanding of paradise. The untouched earth itself is viewed as the ultimate paradise, and humans should live their lives with that as their goal. According to this view, it's a good thing that people are starting to have fewer children; the garden would return to paradise a lot faster if it had fewer (or even no) humans in it.

For some people, this idea of regrowing the garden doesn't go far enough, as the world would still be ruled by death, disease, and human limitation. Our real goal should be to escape the garden entirely by building our own virtual utopia. According to this latest garden narrative, Homo sapiens has won the Game of Life and achieved the historic moment where our technology has put us in the driver's seat of the cosmos. No longer are we relegated to the back seat, subject to the whims of the deterministic and random forces driving the universe. Transhumanists believe that the era of evolution is at an end and that natural selection is being replaced by intelligent design—us.[2] We now possess the technology to steer our future and even transcend our biology. Rather than harvesting the garden or regrowing the garden, adherents to this philosophy believe that humans should focus on developing the technology necessary to escape the limitations of the garden and build a paradise where we can custom-design ourselves, our children, and even our friends. For this master race, every problem that humanity faces will be overcome. It's a technological garden in which the blind receive sight, the lame walk, the deaf hear, and even the dead will be raised to new life when their consciousness is uploaded to the cloud. It will be a virtual paradise of our making.

GOD'S GARDEN

The Bible is a history lesson that warns where each of these paradise narratives will lead—not to a utopia but to a dystopia.

The Bible has something quite different to say about what paradise is and, thus, how humans should live. When we read the story of Genesis carefully, we find that human flourishing is found not in the garden itself but rather in who was in the garden. In the garden, there was God and there was us. Relationship.

Humanity lived in right relationship with God and each other—that's what made it paradise. Yes, we can work hard and achieve great things and enjoy the bounty of the earth, but that's not paradise. Yes, God's creation is beautiful and should be cared for, but not because it is paradise itself. Yes, having hope that looks beyond death and disease is right, but having better bodies and living forever isn't paradise. Instead, the Bible tells us that true paradise comes through being in right relationship with God and each other. That is something that harvesting, regrowing, or escaping the garden can't fix.

The truth is, we intuitively know that the key to paradise is relationship. I learned this as a kid during my first experience at summer camp. The camp I went to was a true wonderland of outdoor beauty. It had great food, its own lake, and the most incredible activities. The brochure made it seem like heaven on earth, the best week a little boy could hope for. Turns out, it was the worst summer of my life. All of the other kids had come to camp with their best bud and had no interest in making a new friend. I spent a week alone and being made fun of. It didn't matter that the woods were beautiful or that I got to go canoeing, swimming, and fishing. Camp sucked. As an adult, I have found that the opposite is also true. I have traveled to some difficult places on earth, places of poverty, disease, and even war. Nobody would make a brochure advertising those places. Yet during those trips, I had some of the most enriching, rewarding, and even fun times of my life because of who I was traveling with. Relationships trump circumstances.

The same principle rings true when it comes to the quantity

of our friends, doesn't it? There have been times in my life when I had more than a thousand friends on social media and still felt totally alone. There have been other times in my life when I had only a few close friends and felt totally understood and fulfilled. It's not just about having relationships, it's the quality of those relationships that matters.

The same is true with God. Throughout this book, I have emphasized that humanity was created for relationship with God. Yet it isn't just any kind of relationship God desires with us. Having a T-shirt or laptop sticker with some cheesy religious slogan doesn't signify a close relationship with God. Neither does showing up to church on Christmas and Easter. That's akin to being Facebook-only friends. A right relationship with God is about more than just keeping tabs on each other's lives from a distance. So how do we do that? How do we know what a quality relationship should look like? This is where morality comes in. Morality is what God has told us about how to have quality relationships, whether between us and God or between us and other people. Morality is borne out of our seeing the reality of who God is and who we are as humans, and then living in light of that truth.

FRIENDSHIP POLICE

After God created the garden of Eden, he told Adam that humans would flourish within this garden if they trusted him. Trust was essential because in the middle of the garden was a tree called the Tree of the Knowledge of Good and Evil. God told Adam that he could eat any of the delicious fruits in the garden except from that one tree. If he ate from that tree, he would die. From the moment that God told them about the tree, Adam and Eve had a choice. They could either trust God or not. It was that simple.

Have you ever wondered why God would plant a tree in paradise that they couldn't eat from? Sometimes it seems like things would have gone a lot better for everybody if God had just forgotten to plant that one or built a tall fence around it or something. After all, if God is all knowing, he would have known that Adam and Eve would choose evil; if God is all good, he wouldn't want them to experience evil; and if God is all powerful, he could have stopped them from choosing evil, right? This is the same reasoning behind the question I was asked in prison: "Why did God allow me to kill three people?" If he's really God—all knowing, all good, and all powerful—why didn't he do anything?

In answering this question, it's important to remember what God emphasized in paradise: relationship. What God wants most and created us for is to love us and have us love him in return. If relationship is what God is really after, then the Tree of the Knowledge of Good and Evil is essential. It wouldn't have been paradise *without* that tree. The tree indicates that what Adam and Eve had in the garden was a real relationship with God, which is built on trust and the choice necessary for true relationship.

Everyone understands that a civilized society requires both laws and a police force to make sure people obey those laws. However, there are also many bad things that are not against the law, like lying to your best friend, gossiping about them, and not showing up to their birthday party. It is perfectly legal to be a jerk. Now, imagine a world in which all of your relationships are under the watchful eye of the Best Friend Forever Police (BFFP). When your birthday rolls around, you send out invitations, get a bunch of snacks, and prep for a great time. Everybody shows up, except your best bro. He RSVP'd, but now it turns out that he has gone behind your back, told everybody that your party is going to be boring, and is a no-show. No worries: just call the BFFP! Before you know it, there will be a knock at your door and an officer will escort your BFF into the party. Problem solved, right? Of course not. How fun would that party be? Would you feel joy having your friend there? It doesn't feel good to know that someone is forced to spend time with you. Love isn't born of compulsion.

The Best Friend Forever Police is a silly example, but I'm betting that you've experienced the pain of someone trying to police a relationship. It's a surefire way to destroy the whole thing. The problem with policing friendship is that it destroys the trust that is necessary for the relationship to flourish. If I'm afraid that I'll be sued or imprisoned for not showing up to a birthday party, I'll go, but not because I want to. My presence at the party will be as fake as the relationship. No one wants a friend who's not really a friend. The truth is that developing genuine relationships requires that we have the freedom to be a jerk.

God desires real relationships with us, which means that evil must be a real possibility. The depth of relationship between two people will always be proportional to the measure of freedom between them. It's why we call the affection that arises between hostages and their kidnappers Stockholm syndrome instead of true love. The depth and richness of relationship that God desires with us explains the level of freedom that he gave us, which in turn explains the depth of evil we are capable of. The Tree of the Knowledge of Good and Evil highlights the trust that is necessary for authentic relationship, but also the consequences of breaking that trust. In Eve's conversation with the serpent, we see how distrust erodes her and Adam's view of God and prompts their following actions.

TROJAN BAGELS

Genesis doesn't give a lot of details but explains that one day in the garden along came a serpent. Although Adam and Eve are together, when the serpent speaks he addresses Eve. He starts the conversation by twisting God's words, asking, "Did God really say, 'You must not eat from any tree in the garden'?"[3] Eve recognizes the serpent's distortion and corrects him. Yet her response reveals that she has already begun to confuse God's love with God's law. She replies, "We may eat fruit from the trees in the garden, but God did say, 'You must not eat fruit from the tree that is in the middle of the garden, and you must not touch it, or you will die.'"[4] What Eve says is partly true—God did tell them not to eat the fruit of that tree—but he didn't say anything about touching it. Eve added that part on her own. It seems she is starting to imagine that she can earn God's favor by adding to his law, by being extra obedient. Adding to God's law leads to legalism, and Eve's response here indicates that she was being legalistic.

There have been times in my life when I have followed Eve's example. Before I placed my trust in Jesus, I lived my life running as far as I could away from God's commands. Then when I became a Christian, my pendulum swung from lawlessness to legalism. I wanted to show God how devoted I was, so I tried my best to be extra good. For example, as a non-Christian, I drank alcohol regularly, but as soon as I became a Christian, I stopped drinking completely. I quit not because I wanted to but because I thought that not drinking was one of God's rules and that the more rules I followed, the happier God would be with me.

I stuck my nose in the air and looked down on all of those less devoted heathens who drank, including my roommate in college. Naturally, my roommate felt judged by my haughty attitude, and so he made it his mission to spite me. He made sure there was plenty of beer in our fridge, just to annoy me, and he would come up with elaborate ways for me to unknowingly ingest alcohol. One day, he skipped class to test his culinary prowess by making some homemade bagels. When I got home later, I was greeted by the sweet aroma of baking and my roommate holding a plate of warm bagels. When I was two bites into that Trojan bagel, he smiled innocently and asked, "Do you like it?" "Oh yeah," I murmured between bites, "it's great." At that, his smile turned devious and a sinister cackle escaped his lips. "Those are beer bagels!" he crowed. "I made them with beer!" Placing the half-eaten bagel down, I walked silently to my room.

In many ways, following and adding to God's rules is what I thought being a good Christian was all about. Devoting myself to a laundry list of dos and don'ts, some that God gave us and many that I invented, allowed me to see myself as a more committed Christian than others, and I lorded it over them. My rule-following was motivated not by love for God and relationship with him but by my pride. I didn't understand the true purpose of morality and saw it only as a way to earn points with God.

MR. YUK

After questioning God's rules and exposing Eve's distorted view of God's love, the serpent calls into question God's wisdom and goodness. He says to Eve, "You will not certainly die. For God knows that when you eat from it your eyes will be opened, and you will be like God, knowing good and evil."[5] In other words, God doesn't know what he's talking about, and he certainly isn't good.

Like Eve, questioning God's wisdom is something I find myself doing more often than I care to admit. In my time as a pastor, I have counseled and supported families that have lost loved ones through disease, tragic accidents, suicide, and murder. I have sat with women and men who have opened up about being abused, molested, and raped. I've sat beside hurting people and found myself at a loss as to what to say. We can pray and pray and yet . . . nothing. Terrible suffering leaves us groping to understand God's wisdom and goodness in it all.

Likewise, many people, myself included, have trouble trusting that God is good and that we can trust his judgment. We question his character and in so doing elevate our own. This is often our gut reaction when we think about hell, isn't it? We think about how bad the existence of hell makes us feel, and we don't trust that God will do what is right, not like we would if we were in charge. Our view of God can become so distorted that we deceive ourselves into believing that we are better than God.

This temptation to follow in Eve's footsteps and question God's wisdom and goodness becomes critical when we think about morality. After all, we have to call into question the character of the lawgiver before we break their laws. If we believe that someone is wise and good and loves us, we'll gladly follow their rules, because we know doing so will lead to our good. Yet we so often have the wrong view of God. We don't understand that God's law flows from his character.

Let me be very clear on this point: God is not primarily concerned about his law. God is concerned about me and you. It's because God loves us that he has given us his law, not the other way around. The Ten Commandments are not for God's sake; they are for ours. It was from God's relational nature and his desire for Adam and Eve's relational good that he commanded, "Don't eat that."

A lot of people misunderstand this aspect of God. Yes, God has rules, but they are to serve as a warning to keep us from harm. God's rules are like signposts in a dark forest that indicate where the path is. You can stray from the path, if you choose, but you will get lost. Follow the path and you're sure to reach your destination. My point is that the markers are not arbitrary, nor are they designed to restrict you. Instead, they are there to guide you.

To change the analogy, we can also think of God's law like

the skull and crossbones symbol printed on a box of detergent. If you were an American kid in the '80s like I was, you'll remember Mr. Yuk stickers instead. They showed a sour-looking face with its tongue sticking out. Both of those symbols were meant to warn and protect kids from dangerous substances. When my kids were really little, my wife and I knew that the skull and crossbones sticker wasn't enough, and so I installed childproof locks on the doors of the cleaning-supplies cabinet. We did this because we loved them and didn't want them to drink poison. Yet as the kids got older and started pitching in around the house, we realized that you can't lock cabinet doors forever. Our kids needed to trust us when we said not to ingest the cleaning supplies. They could have questioned our character, concluding that we were parents obsessed with rules or that we were not telling the truth or that we wanted the cabinet's contents all for ourselves. But their lack of trust would have been mistaken.

Of course, not all parents are loving, wise, or good. Once, my mom convinced me to get a perm because it would give me thick, wavy hair. She loved me and she was a good mom, but her wisdom needed some work. I did not get the wavy hair I was promised. Turns out, my mom was no perm expert and she made the curlers too tight. They were so tight, my bangs broke right off! That's right, I ended up with less hair than I started with, and what I did have was so curly it was plastered to my scalp. So much for thick and wavy. That was a character-building moment for a ten-year-old. The kids at school called me Raggedy Andy for a couple of months, and I was forced to wear a hat because I looked so hideous. My mom loved me desperately, but she failed me hard.

Human parents fail, but God doesn't. God is perfectly loving, perfectly wise, and perfectly good. You can always trust God. So, do you?

Adam and Eve made their decision. They ate the forbidden fruit. In the end, their perspective of God's character had been stripped of its love, wisdom, and goodness. God was no longer God. Eve ate the fruit, Adam followed, and the world changed. This rebellious act brought evil and death into the world. Relationships were broken, and God's image, which should be reflected perfectly in humans, was obscured. God became less to humans, and as a result, we make ourselves and each other less as well—a godless world leading straight to a dehumanizing world.

JUST TRUST ME

When the Q&A time at the prison wrapped up, the chaplain and guards seemed to magically reappear. One by one the prisoners were taken to their cells, and I was led back through the maze of corridors and out the locked front doors. On our drive home, I told the chaplain how impressed I was by John and asked whether he knew anything else about his story. Before he met Jesus, the chaplain said, John was a violent man. He had been a gang member and was known as the Enforcer. Considering the John I had just met, this was difficult to believe. However, a few weeks after speaking at the prison, I received a letter from John in the mail. He wanted to explain the transformation that had taken place in his life after placing his trust in God, and so he had written out his life story for me.

The story he wrote was of a man so wrapped up with himself and consumed by anger that he lost sight of everything and everyone. It was while he was awaiting trial for the murder of two people that John finally cried out for help. He knew that he was guilty of his crimes and that he deserved a prison sentence, but John was seeking a different kind of freedom altogether. He cried out for God to forgive him and heal him of his anger. God answered that prayer. Through Jesus, John began to see God correctly and, subsequently, to see himself correctly for the very first time. By the end of the letter, John explained that he was a new man. Although he was sentenced to life in prison, John knew that God loved him and could mend him and even use him in that prison. By the time I met John, he had been serving Jesus in prison for nine years.

In a world without God, the kind of change that happened in John's life isn't possible. In a determined universe, you may not be responsible for your crimes, but you are defined by them. Without God, you are what you are made of, just star stuff, and you are forever bound to the actions your molecules take. There is no getting around it: in that kind of world, John murdered because he *is* a murderer. It's a dehumanizing world without hope.

In the Christian worldview, you are never defined by what you do. Instead, you are defined by what Jesus did.

As discussed in chapter 6, the Bible explains that Jesus is the image of God and the exact copy of his nature. Those passages emphasize that Jesus is the Son of God—perfectly divine. However, the Bible teaches that Jesus is not only divine; he is also the Son of Man—perfectly human. Jesus fulfilled the purpose of humanity perfectly. He showed us the way that humans should live by trusting God. He lived in right relationship with God and people, even when it cost him his life.

Jesus showed us the love of God by humbling himself and taking on human form, coming to the earth as a baby born in a stable in Bethlehem. Unlike Adam and Eve, Jesus lived out his humanity perfectly, always trusting the love, wisdom, and goodness of God. Jesus never questioned the character of God, nor did he lose sight of the image of God in people. He lived a morally perfect life. He never dehumanized others. Instead he humanized by becoming a servant, devoting his life to loving others and teaching them the truth about who God is and who we are.

Jesus confirmed the wisdom of God when he suffered and gave his life for us on a cross. Though he was blameless, he was whipped, beaten, and mocked. He took our evil on himself, accepting the death that we deserve so that, through him, death could be defeated. People tried to make Jesus both less human and less divine by murdering him in the most demeaning of manners, but Jesus never retaliated. Instead, he proved the goodness of God with his last breaths as he forgave those who were murdering him, saying, "Father, forgive them, for they do not know what they are doing."[6] Three days after his death, Jesus rose from the dead, demonstrating his power over the grave and extending grace and forgiveness to us.

When we place our trust in the love, wisdom, and goodness of God, demonstrated in Jesus, our relationship with God is repaired. We are no longer defined by the choices of our past. Instead, Jesus offers us his identity as our own. In him, our humanity is being restored. Only in Jesus are we truly free to be fully human with the purpose, value, and flourishing that we were made for.

BECOMING PERFECT

In Colossians, Paul explains a key concept concerning our humanity. Paul writes of Jesus, "He is the one we proclaim, admonishing and teaching everyone with all wisdom, so that we may present everyone perfect in Christ. To this end I strenuously contend with all the energy Christ so powerfully works in me."[7] This was Paul's work: to help people fully flourish. He understood that this takes place only in Jesus.

The word *perfect* is often misunderstood as some unattainable ideal. Paul's desire to "present everyone perfect in Christ" refers back to God's design in the garden. In the Greek, the word *perfect* (*teleios*) derives from the root word *purpose* (*telos*). Thus, perfect in this context means something that completely fulfills the purpose it was designed for.

We still use it this way in English. For example, I was once working on my car and needed to replace my brake rotor. Attempting to remove the rotor, I tried loosening a large shaft bolt that held the bearings. I went to the auto parts store three times trying to find the right socket, until I ran out of time and patience. It ended up that the socket was specialized, so, fingers crossed, I ordered what appeared to be the correct one online and waited for it to arrive. I was optimistic as I pulled the socket out of the packaging and ran out to the car to try it. My wife followed me out and asked, "Is it the right one?" I called out, "It's perfect!"

The way I used the word perfect in that context gets at the idea that Paul is communicating. By calling the socket perfect, I was saying that it was perfectly designed for removing that exact bolt. Once I had the perfect socket, I learned why that bolt was so unique—it didn't need to come off! After I removed the nut, it became apparent that it was not connected with the rotor at all. The rotor was simply rusty and needed some encouraging taps with a mallet to come off. It was one of those humbling moments, which I seem to have often. As I put that specialized socket into my toolbox, I consoled myself with the thought that one day it will be perfectly suited for replacing the bearings.

Now, consider what Paul is saying. Jesus is perfectly suited, when we place our trust in him, to fulfill the purpose that God created humanity for. The purpose of humanity, true flourishing, is to be in right relationship with God and people—that's what both life now and the life to come are all about.

John's gospel records a prayer that Jesus prays right before he is betrayed and murdered. Jesus prays, "Now this is eternal life: that they know you, the only true God, and Jesus Christ, whom you have sent."[8] According to Jesus, paradise isn't about riches or merely living forever, it's about being in loving relationship forever. The flip side of that, broken relationship forever, is hell. That's why Jesus so often warned people about hell. Broken relationship is not something he wanted, and it's not what we were created for. When speaking about heaven and hell, Jesus' use of metaphor always points to something greater. Heaven, loving relationship forever, is more beautiful than our minds can conceive. Likewise, hell, broken relationship forever, is worse than we can imagine. If humanization and dehumanization have taught us anything, it's that these are realities we don't need to die to get a taste of. We can begin to experience heaven on earth, right relationship, or hell on earth, broken relationship, starting now. So which do you want?

In John 8:36, Jesus says, "So if the Son sets you free, you will be free indeed." That's what I want: to be truly free—free to be human. The true glory of a thing is when it is free to do exceedingly well at what it was made for. We were made to be loved by God, to love him, and to love each other for eternity. This is what it means to be perfectly human.

ACKNOWLEDGMENTS

Writing a book is a collaborative process that requires a team of gifted people. I want to acknowledge and thank the following people:

Chris Battle
Christina Bergstresser
Jake Bergen
Lisa Brechbiel
Maty Brechbiel
Tate Brechbiel
Melissa Campbell
Terry Crosby
Marj Drury
Andrew Grosso
DJ Hiebert
Marj Hiebert
Lee Jong-rak
Steve Kim

Jeandré Knauber
Rachel MacKenzie
Daniel Markin
Kyle Meeker
Jon Morrison
Lexii Ratzlaff
Suphannee Saengseengam (Noi)
Mel and Jenny Spielman
Mark Sweeney
Nancy Steiger
Richard Szmutko
Derrick Uittenbosch
The wonderful team at Zondervan

NOTES

Chapter 1: Digital Genocide

1. The short films from the series played in film festivals around the world, winning a number of awards, including Best Short Film, Best Documentary Short, Best Foreign Short, and a People's Choice Award (www.thehumanproject.ca).
2. Anisa Subedar, "The Country Where Facebook Posts Whipped Up Hate," *BBC*, 12 September 2018, https://bbc.com/news /blogs-trending-45449938.
3. Steve Stecklow, "Why Facebook Is Losing the War on Hate Speech in Myanmar," *Reuters*, 15 August 2018, https://www. reuters.com/investigates/special-report/myanmar-facebook-hate/.
4. *Auschwitz: The Nazis and "The Final Solution,"* dir. Laurence Rees and Catherine Tatge, BBC, 2005.
5. Claudia Koonz, *The Nazi Conscience* (Cambridge, Mass.: Harvard Univ. Press, 2003), 273.
6. *Auschwitz,* emphasis added.
7. David Livingstone Smith, *Less Than Human: Why We Demean, Enslave, and Exterminate Others* (New York: St. Martin's Press, 2011), 2, emphasis in original.
8. Philip Zimbardo, *The Lucifer Effect: Understanding How Good People Turn Evil* (New York: Random House, 2007), 16.
9. James 3:7–10.
10. Russell Peters, *Nobody Likes Mondays,* YouTube, https://www .youtube.com/watch?v=nnc6Asflzq8, accessed September 2019.
11. Ben Zimmer, "How Did 'Monday' Become a Racist Slur?" *Boston Globe,* 29 July 2012, https://www.bostonglobe.com /ideas/2012/07/28/how-did-monday-become-racist-slur-how-did

-monday-become-racist-slur/Mf4fQEVcXabGKHFaDMZ4NO
/story.html.

12. Jon Ronson, *So You've Been Publicly Shamed* (New York: Riverhead, 2015), 68.
13. Lindy West, *Shrill: Notes from a Loud Woman* (New York: Hachette, 2016), 254.
14. Zimbardo, *Lucifer Effect,* 16.
15. Hannah Arendt, *Eichmann in Jerusalem: A Report on the Banality of Evil* (New York: Penguin, 2006), 276.
16. Slavenka Drakulić, *They Would Never Hurt a Fly: War Criminals on Trial in the Hague* (New York: Viking Penguin, 2005), 190–91, emphasis in original.
17. Ronson, *So You've Been Publicly Shamed,* 246–47.
18. James Dobson, *Fatal Addiction: Ted Bundy's Final Interview with Dr. James Dobson,* VHS, 1989.
19. Smith, *Less Than Human,* 273.

Chapter 2: Caged Bird in Bangkok

1. Elin Kelsey, *You Are Stardust* (Montreal: Owlkids, 2012).
2. Charles M. Bakewell, *Source Book in Ancient Philosophy* (New York: Charles Scribner's Sons, 1907), 60.
3. Michael Polanyi, *Personal Knowledge: Towards a Post-Critical Philosophy* (Chicago: Univ. of Chicago Press, 1962), 142.
4. William Seabrook, *The Magic Island* (1929; New York: Dover, 2016), 101–2, emphasis in original.
5. Yuval Noah Harari, *Sapiens: A Brief History of Humankind* (Toronto: McClelland and Stewart, 2014), 391–92, emphasis in original.
6. Harari, *Sapiens,* 110.
7. Mark 12:28–31.
8. Luke 10:25–37.

Chapter 3: Furbabies

1. Katie Cowell, "What Role Does Your Dog Play in the Family?" *Just Right by Purina,* 12 July 2018, https://www.justrightpet food.com/blog/dogs-are-family-survey.
2. Carley Lintz, "New Insights on Millennial Pet Owners," *Pet*

Business, 27 February 2018, http://www.petbusiness.com /New-Insights-on-Millennial-Pet-Owners/.

3. Yuval Noah Harari, *Sapiens: A Brief History of Humankind* (Toronto: McClelland and Stewart, 2014), 109.

4. Wesley J. Smith, *A Rat Is a Pig Is a Dog Is a Boy: The Human Cost of the Animal Rights Movement* (New York: Encounter Books, 2012).

5. David Teather, "'Holocaust on a Plate' Angers US Jews," *Guardian,* 3 March 2003, https://www.theguardian.com /media/2003/mar/03/advertising.marketingandpr.

6. Peter Singer, "All Animals Are Equal," in *Contemporary Moral Problems,* 10th ed., ed. James E. White (Boston: Wadsworth, 2012), 284.

7. Andy Bannister, Justin Trottier, and Justin Brierley, *Foundations for Human Rights: A Christian and a Humanist in Conversation,* Apologetics Canada Conference, 2018, 33:35–36:28, https:// www.youtube.com/watch?v=fnNSUI2KW0E.

8. Adam Hochschild, *King Leopold's Ghost* (New York: Mariner Books, 1998), 169.

9. Hochschild, *King Leopold's Ghost,* 145.

10. Pamela Newkirk, *Spectacle: The Astonishing Life of Ota Benga* (New York: HarperCollins, 2015), 33.

11. Aristotle, *Politics,* trans. Benjamin Jowett (New York: Dover, 2000), 27.

12. Charles Darwin, *The Descent of Man* (London: Penguin, 2004), 167.

13. Darwin, *Descent of Man,* 167.

14. Darwin, *Descent of Man,* 183.

15. *Buck v. Bell,* 274 U.S. 200 (1927).

16. George William Hunter, *Civic Biology* (New York: American Book Company, 1914), 196.

17. Madison Grant, *The Passing of the Great Race: Or the Racial Basis of European History,* 3rd ed. (n.c.: Ostara Publications, 2016).

18. Stefan Kühl, *The Nazi Connection: Eugenics, American Racism, and German National Socialism* (New York: Oxford Univ. Press, 1994), 37.

19. Jon Ronson, *The Men Who Stare at Goats* (New York: Simon and Schuster, 2004), 175.

20. Cahal Milmo, "Fury at DNA Pioneer's Theory: Africans Are Less Intelligent Than Westerners," *Independent,* 17 October 2007, https://www.independent.co.uk/news/science/fury-at -dna-pioneers-theory-africans-are-less-intelligent-than -westerners-394898.html.

21. *American Masters: Decoding Watson,* dir. Mark Mannucci, PBS, 2 January 2019.

22. Brian Resnick, "The Dark Psychology of Dehumanization, Explained," *Vox,* 7 March 2017, https://www.vox.com /science-and-health/2017/3/7/14456154/dehumanization -psychology-explained.

23. Amy Harmon, "James Watson Had a Chance to Salvage His Reputation on Race. He Made Things Worse," *New York Times,* 1 January 2019, https://www.nytimes.com/2019/01/01 /science/watson-dna-genetics-race.html.

24. Yuval Noah Harari, *Homo Deus: A Brief History of Tomorrow* (New York: HarperCollins, 2017), 258–59.

25. Harari, *Homo Deus,* 351.

Chapter 4: She Has a Hole in Her Heart

1. "A Universal Declaration of Human Rights," n.d., https://www .un.org/en/ga/search/view_doc.asp?symbol=A/RES/217(III).

2. Jacques Maritain, introduction to *Human Rights: Comments and Interpretations,* United Nations Educational, Scientific and Cultural Organization (Paris, 25 July 1948), https://unesdoc .unesco.org/ark:/48223/pf0000155042, emphasis in original.

3. Gen. 2:7.

4. Chaim Stern, *Gates of Prayer: The New Union Prayerbook; Weekdays, Sabbaths, and Festivals* (New York: Central Conference of American Rabbis, 1975), 240.

5. Exodus 32.

6. Kenneth Feinberg, "What Is the Value of a Human Life?" *This I Believe* series, NPR, 25 May 2008, https://www.npr.org /templates/story/story.php?storyId=90760725.

7. Chris Jones, "Kenneth Feinberg: The Nation's Leading Expert in Picking Up the Pieces," *Esquire,* 16 December 2013, https://

www.esquire.com/news-politics/a26408/kenneth-feinberg
-interview-0114/.

8. Feinberg, "What Is the Value of a Human Life?"

9. Peter Garnsey, *Ideas of Slavery from Aristotle to Augustine*
   (New York: Cambridge Univ. Press, 1999), 81–82.

10. Mahatma Gandhi, "A Letter Addressed to the Director-General
    of UNESCO," in *Human Rights: Comments and Interpretations*.

11. Adam Hochschild, *King Leopold's Ghost: A Story of Greed,
    Terror, and Heroism in Colonial Africa* (New York: Mariner
    Books, 1998), 112.

12. "Report on Industrial Schools for Indians and Half-Breeds,"
    14 March 1879, http://bcmetis.com/wp-content/uploads
    /IndustrialSchoolsReport.pdf, 12.

13. National Archives of Canada, Record Group 10, vol. 6810,
    file 470–2–3, vol. 7, 55 (L-3) and 63 (N-3).

Chapter 5: Lonely Planet

1. Denise Winterman, "Taste and Smell: What Is It Like to Live
   without Them?" BBC News, 29 June 2013, https://www.bbc
   .com/news/magazine-23051270.

2. Darrell Bricker and John Ibbitson, *Empty Planet: The Shock
   of Global Population Decline* (New York: Broadway Books,
   2019).

3. Mentos National Night, https://www.youtube.com/watch?v=8jx
   U89x78ac.

4. Orna Donath, "Regretting Motherhood: A Sociopolitical
   Analysis," *The University of Chicago Press Journals* 40, no. 2
   (2015): 356.

5. Jean Mackenzie, "The Mothers Who Regret Having Children,"
   BBC News, 3 April 2018, https://www.bbc.com/news
   /education-43555736.

6. Donath, "Regretting Motherhood," 356.

7. Mark Tran, "Girl Starved to Death While Parents Raised
   Virtual Child in Online Game," *Guardian*, 5 March 2010,
   https://www.theguardian.com/world/2010/mar/05/korean-girl
   -starved-online-game.

8. Gatebox—Promotion Movie "Okaeri"_english, https://www
   .youtube.com/watch?v=nkcKaNqfykg.

9. "CREEPER Act of 2017," Pub. L. No. H.R. 4655 (n.d.), https://www.congress.gov/bill/115th-congress/house-bill/4655.

10. Tara John, "How the World's First Loneliness Minister Will Tackle 'the Sad Reality of Modern Life,'" *Time*, 25 April 2018, https://time.com/5248016/tracey-crouch-uk-loneliness-minister/.

11. Charlotte S. Yeh, "The Power and Prevalence of Loneliness," Harvard Health Publishing, 13 January 2017, https://www.health.harvard.edu/blog/the-power-and-prevalence-of-loneliness-2017011310977.

12. Norimitsu Onishi, "A Generation in Japan Faces a Lonely Death," *New York Times*, 30 November 2017, https://www.nytimes.com/2017/11/30/world/asia/japan-lonely-deaths-the-end.html.

13. Sherry Turkle, *Reclaiming Conversation: The Power of Talk in a Digital Age* (New York: Penguin, 2015), 358–59.

14. Turkle, *Reclaiming Conversation*, 362.

15. Sherry Turkle, *Alone Together: Why We Expect More from Technology and Less from Each Other* (New York: Basic Books, 2012), 1.

16. Turkle, *Alone Together*, 101.

Chapter 6: Human Flavor

1. *The Drop Box*, dir. Brian Ivie, 2014.

2. Matt. 5:13.

3. Alan Torrance, "Discovering the Incarnate Saviour of the World: The Theological Vision of the Torrance Tradition" (lecture, Regent College, Vancouver, March 2006).

4. Col. 1:15.

5. Heb. 1:3.

6. John 1:18.

7. Genesis 12 and 20.

8. The story of King David is found in 1 and 2 Samuel.

9. 1 John 4:8.

10. Richard of St. Victor, *Richard of St. Victor: The Twelve Patriarchs; The Mystical Ark; Book Three of the Trinity*, ed. Grover A. Zinn, The Classics of Western Spirituality (New York: Paulist, 1979), 47–48.

11. Gen. 2:20.

12. Matt. 5:13.
13. Matt. 6:21.
14. Matt. 5:11.
15. Matt. 5:39.
16. Rom. 5:2–4.
17. Rom. 8:18.
18. 2 Cor. 12:10.

Chapter 7: Of Weddings and Funerals

1. Ps. 23:4 ESV.
2. Charles Darwin, *The Descent of Man* (London: Penguin Classics, 2004), 120.
3. Steven Pinker, "The Moral Instinct," *New York Times Magazine*, 13 January 2008.
4. Sam Harris, *Letter to a Christian Nation* (New York: Vintage, 2006), 50–51, emphasis in original.
5. Sam Harris, *Free Will* (New York: Free Press, 2012), 5, emphasis in original.
6. Pierre-Simon, Marquis de Laplace, *A Philosophical Essay on Probabilities,* trans. Frederick Wilson (New York: John Wiley and Sons, 2015), 12.
7. Peter Pringle, *The Murder of Nikolai Vavilov: The Story of Stalin's Persecution of One of the Great Scientists of the Twentieth Century* (New York: Simon and Schuster, 2008).
8. David Kyle Johnson, *Exploring Metaphysics,* DVD, vol. 1 (The Great Courses, 2014).
9. Stephen Cave, "There's No Such Thing as Free Will: But We're Better Off Believing in It Anyway," *Atlantic,* June 2016, https://www.theatlantic.com/magazine/archive/2016/06/theres-no-such-thing-as-free-will/480750/.
10. Johnson, *Exploring Metaphysics.*
11. For a good account of the Leopold and Loeb story, see Simon Baatz, *For the Thrill of It: Leopold, Loeb, and the Murder That Shocked Jazz Age Chicago* (New York: HarperCollins, 2008).
12. "All Life Is a Series of Infinite Chances," Famous Trials, https://famous-trials.com/leopoldandloeb/1707-infinitechances.
13. Viktor E. Frankl, *Man's Search for Meaning* (Boston: Beacon Press, 2006), 132, emphasis in original.

Chapter 8: Skull and Crossbones

1. Andy Steiger, *Thinking? Answering Life's Five Biggest Questions* (Abbotsford: Apologetics Canada Publishing, 2015).
2. For a detailed exploration of transhumanism, see Ray Kurzweil, *The Singularity Is Near: When Humans Transcend Biology* (New York: Penguin, 2005); Max Tegmark, *Life 3.0: Being Human in the Age of Artificial Intelligence* (New York: Knopf, 2017); Jessica Riskin, *The Restless Clock: A History of the Centuries-Old Argument over What Makes Living Things Tick* (Chicago: Univ. of Chicago Press, 2016).
3. Gen. 3:1.
4. Gen. 3:2–3.
5. Gen. 3:4–5.
6. Luke 23:34.
7. Col. 1:28–29 (NIV 1984).
8. John 17:3.